Integrating Multicultural Literature

In Libraries and Classrooms in Secondary Schools

KaaVonia Hinton
and
Gail K. Dickinson

Linworth Books

Professional Development Resources for
K-12 Library Media and Technology Specialists

Library of Congress Cataloging-in-Publication Data

Hinton, KaaVonia, 1973-
 Integrating multicultural literature in libraries and classrooms in secondary
schools / KaaVonia Hinton and Gail K. Dickinson.
    p. cm.
 Includes bibliographical references and index.
 ISBN 1-58683-218-2 (pbk.)

 1. American literature--Minority authors--Study and teaching (Secondary) 2.
Ethnic groups--United States--Intellectual life--Study and teaching (Secondary)
3. Minorities--United States--Intellectual life--Study and teaching (Secondary) 4.
Young adult literature, American--Study and teaching (Secondary) 5. Young
adult literature, American--Bibliography. 6. High school students--Books and
reading--United States. 7. School librarian participation in curriculum planning--
United States. 8. Multicultural education--United States. I. Dickinson, Gail K.
II. Title.

 PS153.M56H56 2007
 810.9'928208693--dc22

                              2007000188

Cynthia Anderson: Acquisitions Editor
Carol Simpson: Editorial Director
Judi Repman: Consulting Editor

Published by Linworth Publishing, Inc.
3650 Olentangy River Road, Suite 250
Columbus, Ohio 43214

ISBN: 1-58683-218-2

5 4 3 2 1

Table of Contents

Table of Contents *continued*

Table of Contents *continued*

Table of Contents continued

Table of Contents *continued*

Introduction

M iddle and high school students are beginning to find their place in the world around them. Through music, video, and other media in popular culture, there is a wealth of opportunity to integrate multicultural resources into the secondary classroom as well as the school library. While there are several excellent resources available for teachers and librarians in elementary schools, there are few that suggest ways to use multicultural resources in middle schools, and fewer for high schools. This book will fill that void by suggesting specific multicultural materials along with specific ways of using them in the secondary school classroom.

The books in these chapters were compiled from award lists and the authors' research and work as book critics. The titles were published over the last fifteen years and chosen because of their proven success with students in the authors' classrooms and in classrooms across the United States as reported in various anecdotal reports and research studies. However, there are exceptions. We included older titles such as, Maxine Hong Kingston's *The Woman Warrior: Memoirs of a Girlhood Among Ghosts* (1976), N. Scott Momaday's *House Made of Dawn* (1968), and Nancy Garden's *Annie on My Mind* (1982), because we believe such titles are "classics."

Each chapter contains a brief introduction of the section followed by *Integrating Multicultural Texts* features that provide a synopsis of three to five texts from many genres—film, poetry, picture books, short stories—and several research-based activities. An annotated list of additional texts concludes each chapter. Some of the books in a particular chapter could also be included in other chapters. For example, we cite *Cool Salsa* edited by Lori Carlson in our chapter titled "Language/Country of Origin" though we realize it could be discussed there or in chapter 4, "Race and Ethnicity."

Read Alike boxes list titles that can be paired or used in text sets because they are similar in theme. *In the Research* features highlight research and literary analyses, particularly those done by librarians and teachers, and other scholarly materials that focus on teaching and exploring multicultural literature, such as interviews with diverse authors. *Collaborative Opportunities* features offer suggestions for teachers and library media specialists.

The tips, suggested activities, and sidebars are written so that substitutions can be made if the school library does not have the books mentioned. A list of online multicultural resources is provided in each chapter as well.

About the Authors

KaaVonia Hinton is an assistant professor in Educational Curriculum and Instruction at Old Dominion University in Norfolk, Virginia. Her work focuses on literacy materials, especially literature for adults, children, and young adults labeled multicultural, critical biographies of black writers, and literary criticism. She is the author of *Angela Johnson: Poetic Prose* (Scarecrow Press, 2006).

Gail K. Dickinson is an associate professor in Educational Curriculum and Instruction at Old Dominion University in Norfolk, Virginia. Her work focuses on school library media programs and services, including collections and budgeting, and National Board Certified Teachers.

Chapter 1

Using Multicultural Literature

What Is Young Adult Literature?

In recent years we have noticed announcements in magazines and journals urging readers to suggest appropriate labels for literature often read by young people in middle, junior high, and high schools. Labels such as adolescent literature, teen fiction, or our favorite, YA (young adult) lit., are inadequate, the periodicals seem to suggest. Scholars, teachers, and librarians use various labels and often disagree on the age of the books' audience. The Young Adult Library Services Association, a division of the American Library Association, describes young adults as youth between the ages of twelve and eighteen. According to Nilsen & Donelson (1993), young adult literature is "anything that readers between the approximate ages of twelve and twenty choose to read (as opposed to what they may be coerced to read for class assignments)" (p. 6). Similarly, some include in the definition of young adult literature books written for and marketed to adults that have young adult appeal such as Mark Haddon's *Curious Incident of the Dog in the Night-Time* (2003) and Toni Morrison's *The Bluest Eye* (1970).

Bucher and Manning (2006) highlight the following characteristics of young adult literature:

> It should reflect young adults' age and development by addressing their reading abilities, thinking levels, and interest levels. It should deal with contemporary issues, problems, and experiences with character to whom adolescents can relate. It should consider contemporary world perspectives including cultural, social, and gender diversity; environmental issues; global politics; and international interdependence. (p. 9)

For the purposes of this book, we define young adult literature primarily as non-"classical" or "canonized" literature of all genres (i.e., poetry, short stories, novels, and picture books) that features protagonists from ages twelve to eighteen, yet canonical literature does have value with this age group as well. Canonical literature is taught in teacher preparation classes and other sources, such as *From Hinton to Hamlet: Building Bridges Between Young Adult Literature and the Classics* by Sarah K. Herz and Donald R. Gallo, review its use in middle and high school.

Uses of Young Adult Literature

Teachers have traditionally viewed young adult literature as inferior to the classics. Our conversations with classroom teachers reveal that many view young adult literature as unsophisticated, poorly written, short, entertaining, and less rigorous. They see little need to give whole class periods over to reading it because students can often understand and relate to the issues and themes addressed in the literature on their own, proving little need for an expert reader's scaffolding of complex ideas. Young adult literature is reserved for outside-school literacy development, book reports, and sustained silent reading.

Over the last few years, several informative texts argued that young adult literature could be used for both pleasurable and critical readings (see Hinton-Johnson, 2003; Moore, 1997; Soter, 1997). Within these texts, scholars use complex literary theories (e.g., Black feminism, deconstruction, New Criticism, and so forth) to emphasize multiple meanings and ways of reading select young adult literature while establishing the validity and intellectual rigor encouraged by critical study of young adult literature (see Hinton-Johnson, 2003; Moore, 1997; Soter, 1997). Multicultural literature for young adults, primarily because of complex social issues and revisionist historical perspectives, can often endure critical scrutiny and requires the guidance of a knowledgeable librarian or teacher.

What Is Multicultural Literature?

A number of debates surround multicultural literature (see Taxel, 1992, 1997; Harris, 1996; Smith, 1997), but one of the main debates reveals disagreement and confusion concerning its definition. Some define it broadly, arguing that everyone "has a cultural heritage, often one that is woven from many diverse strands," and therefore all literature for youth "could be considered culturally diverse in relation to each other" (Cullinan & Galda, 2005, p. 275). While this is undisputable, others argue that such a broad definition of multicultural literature is contrary to the purpose of advocating for the use of multicultural literature in our nation's classrooms. Cai (2002) explains, "...a definition of multicultural literature should...draw a demarcation line between the literature of the dominant mainstream culture and that of marginalized cultures. If multicultural literature includes all cultures, the term loses its meaning...Without the binary opposition, what is the point of using a different name?" (p. 8).

Cai and Bishop (1994) consider multicultural literature an umbrella term including three types of literature: world literature (literature from non-Western countries and people from the Southern or Eastern Hemispheres), cross-cultural literature (books about interactions between cultures and books written by authors about cultures outside their own), and "minority" literature or literature from parallel cultures (literature written by and about members of the cultural group depicted). In an effort to clarify what is meant by multicultural literature here, we rely on Bishop's (1997) definition. Bishop (1997) defines multicultural literature as works "that reflect the racial, ethnic and social diversity that is characteristic of our pluralistic society and of the world" (p. 3). However, in this book we have limited ourselves primarily to multicultural texts about the experiences of underrepresented groups in the United States. We use the terms "culturally diverse literature" and "culturally relevant literature," in addition to "multicultural literature," interchangeably for variety.

Multicultural Literature in Secondary Schools

While many research efforts have been undertaken to advocate the use of multicultural literature in the classroom, very little research has been done

Multicultural Resources

Online Resources: Indian Boarding Schools

http://www.hanksville.org/sand/intellect/gof.html
http://memory.loc.gov/learn/lessons/01/indian/
http://clarke.cmich.edu/indian/treatyeducation.htm

Other Resources

Teaching African American Literature
edited by M. Graham
Routledge, 1998

Teaching Multicultural Literature in Grades K-8
edited by Violet J. Harris
Christopher-Gordon, 1992

Using Multiethnic Literature in the K-8 Classroom
edited by Violet J. Harris
Christopher-Gordon, 1997

"Guiding Young Readers to Multicultural Literature"
by KaaVonia Hinton-Johnson and Gail Dickinson
Library Media Connection, 23.7, April/May 2005, p. 42-45

Writers of Multicultural Fiction for Young Adults: A Bio-Critical Sourcebook
edited by M. Daphne Kutzer
Greenwood, 1996

A Broken Flute: The Native Experience in Books for Children
edited by Doris Seale and Beverly Slapin
Alta Mira, 2005

on how multicultural literature should be used as a pedagogical tool. The question becomes what does one do with the literature once it is included in the classroom (Soter, 1997). Though the research is not clear on the most effective way to teach multicultural literature so that it is in line with the goals of multicultural education, it does recognize three major approaches:

- Using multicultural literature to obtain literacy
- Viewing multicultural literature as a mirror and/or window for *all* students
- Relying on multicultural literature to bring issues of race, gender, and class to the forefront.

Integrating multicultural literature with content taught in the classroom adds a deeper and richer context to classroom content, therefore intensifying the effect of the three approaches listed above.

Multicultural literature's role in the classroom should be similar to that of any other literature (Bishop, 1994). Traditionally, literature has been used to teach academic skills such as reading and writing (Bishop, 1994; Ford et al., 2000). Students are often encouraged to learn to appreciate literature and enjoy reading it. Moreover, teachers want students to recognize good literature and separate it from literature that lacks quality. Scimone's (1999) poetry assignment is an illustration of an activity that encourages students to evaluate literature. Scimone, an English teacher, asked his tenth grade class to create a book of poetry. He hoped his students would get two things out of this assignment: 1) practice evaluating poetic works and 2) interest in and an appreciation of poetry. While Scimone's focus was on teaching students to appreciate, interpret, and evaluate poetry, other teachers use literature to help students become literate.

Several anecdotal reports written by teachers focused on the use of literature to help students improve their reading and writing skills (see, for example, Martin, 1997; O'Malley, 1997; Gunther, 2000; Mayo, 2000). Among the books used were titles written by and about people of color. For instance, Martin (1997) has his students look closely at Alice Walker's craft, particularly the poetic images, the title essay in *In Search of Our Mothers' Gardens*. Moreover, the students were asked to look at Walker's organizational strategy and use of transitional phrases. Finally, the students were asked to respond in writing. Similarly, O'Malley (1997) asks his students to observe characterization, voice, and theme in Sandra Cisneros' *The House on Mango Street* (1984).

Little research reveals that teachers are using multicultural literature in the traditional ways in which literature has been used in the classroom. That is, the literature is not being used to teach literacy skills as "regular" literature has in the past. Instead, a large number of experimental studies and anecdotal reports reveal that teachers, based on the reading material chosen and writing assignments given, assume students are already proficient readers and writers when they introduce them to multicultural literature (see, for example, Athanases, 1996; Bean, Cantu'Valerio, Senior, & White, 1999).

Teachers, scholars, and researchers seem to share Bishop's (1994) belief that books contain the power to provide self-affirmation for some students, while introducing others to new ways of viewing people who are not of their cultural group. Consciously choosing books that mirror students' life experiences help students celebrate diversity, and they speak to students about themselves and the lives of others.

Along with including literature that celebrates diversity, researchers also argue for the inclusion of assignments that validate each student's life experiences and cultural identities (Athanases, Christiano, & Lay, 1995). For example, in an anecdotal study, Athanases et al. (1995) describe how, after a unit in which students read literature about Asians, Asian Americans, and Pacific Islanders, they asked the students to interview people in Oakland's Chinatown to learn "perceptions of life in Chinatown versus life in the homeland" (p. 32).

Despite some opposition, there is considerable evidence in the research literature that suggests issues of race, class, and gender should be discussed when teaching multicultural literature (see, for example, Rhoades, 1991; Greene, 1995; Roman, 1996; Willis, 1997; Glenn-Paul, 1998; Rothenberg, 2000). Sleeter & Grant (1999) argue that while teachers should strive to help students develop appreciation and respect for other cultures, they should also help students understand sociopolitical factors surrounding cultural groups. As Bishop (1994) explains, multicultural literature "offer[s] opportunities to examine critically the society in which we live, and the values and assumptions that underlie conflicts, events, and behaviors" (p. xvi).

Moreover, Bishop (1994) suggests that if books focus on issues such as racism, sexism, and so on, these issues should be discussed with students. Pate (1992) maintains: "Of all the formal agents in society, the schools are in the best position to prevent and reduce prejudice" (p. 137). Pate also offers multicultural literature as an important part of reducing prejudice. Other scholars and researchers seem to agree; they argue that multicultural education is more than sampling from a multicultural "food court" (Rothenberg, 2000) or being engaged in "cultural tourism" (Glenn-Paul, 1998). And, still, others argue that multicultural efforts that avoid discussions of how race, class, and gender gets constructed in society runs the risk of trivializing multicultural education and reinforcing the social inequities that are already in existence (Fang et al., 1999; Rothenberg, 2000).

The Significance of Multicultural Literature

Most agree that literature in general and multicultural literature, in particular, is powerful. Multicultural literature can:

1. Instill pride and self-empowerment in readers

2. Be used as a weapon for fighting racism and other injustices

3. Help students look critically at the world

4. Encourage students to question past, present, and future realities

5. Pass on societal values

6. Promote empathy (Bishop, 1997; Cai, 2002).

Bishop (1992) maintains that students who do not see their culture reflected in the literature they read may believe that they have no value and little or no importance in society and in school. As a result, students may become uninterested in school, and their grades may suffer (Spears-Bunton, 1990). According to Spears-Bunton (1990), African American students may be reading at low levels because of what she calls "a cultural mismatch" between the students and the books they read. Likewise, Menchaca (2000) maintains Hispanic children will do better in school if they are provided with a culturally relevant curriculum. Anaya (1992) echoes this sentiment when he claims "…part of the cause for our alarming dropout statistics is this narrow, circumscribed curriculum in language and literature" (cited in Margerison, 1995, p. 259).

A Word on Cultural Authenticity

Like the definition of multicultural literature, "cultural authenticity" remains an often-debated topic. We recognize the importance and complexity of the arguments around authenticity, but here, our purpose is not to deny that "outsiders" have a right to write about cultural groups other than their own, neither is it to censor authors or to provide as, Lasky (1996) accuses, "…a kind of literary version of ethnic cleansing" (p. 4). However, most of the selections discussed in this book are by individuals who are of or closely aligned with the cultural group they have chosen to write about.

In the Reseach   **Going Beyond the Book**

Page argues that teaching multicultural literature is not enough to promote learning, motivation, or transformation in the language arts classroom. She suggests that in addition to teaching multicultural literature, educators should attempt to do the following in classrooms:

1. Build relationships
2. Establish trust
3. Be honest
4. Be respectful
5. Be helpful
6. Promote social action
7. Have fun

Page, M. L. (2004). Going beyond the book: A multicultural educator in the English language arts classroom. *Voices from the Middle, 12*(1), 8-15.

Works Cited

Athanases, S. Z. (1996). A gay-themed lesson in an ethnic literature curriculum: Tenth graders' responses to "Dear Anita." *Harvard Educational Review*, *66*(2), 231-256.

Athanases, S. Z., Christiano, D., & Lay, E. (1995). Fostering empathy and finding common ground in multiethnic classes. *English Journal*, *84*(3), 26-34.

Bean, T. W., Cantu'Valerio, P., Senior, H. M., & White, F. (1999). Secondary English students' engagement in reading and writing about a multicultural novel. *The Journal of Educational Research, 193*(1), 32-37.

Bishop, R. S. (1992). Children's books in a multicultural world: A view from the USA. In E. Evans (Ed.), *Reading against racism* (pp. 19-38). Buckingham: Open University Press.

Bishop, R. S. (Ed.). (1994). *Kaleidoscope: A multicultural booklist for grades k-8*. Illinois: NCTE.

Bishop, R. S. (1997). Selecting literature for a multicultural curriculum. In V. J. Harris (Ed.), *Using multiethnic literature in the k-8 classroom* (pp. 1-19). Norwood, MA: Christopher-Gordon Publishers, Inc.

Bucher, K. T., & Manning, M. L. (2006). *Young adult literature: Exploration, evaluation, and appreciation*. Boston: Pearson Education.

Cai, M. (2002). *Multicultural literature for children and young adults: Reflections on critical issues*. Westport, CT: Greenwood.

Cai, M., & Bishop, R. S. (1994). Multicultural literature for children: Towards a clarification of the concept. In A. H. Dyson & C. Genishi (Eds.), *The need for story: Cultural diversity in classroom and community* (pp. 57-70). Illinois: NCTE.

Cisneros, S. (1984). *The House on Mango Street*. Houston, TX: Arte Publico.

Cullinan, L., & Galda, B. E. (2005). *Literature and the child*. Belmont, CA: Wadsworth.

Fang, Z., Fu, D., & Lamme, L. L. (1999). Rethinking the role of multicultural literature in literacy instruction: Problems, paradox, and possibilities. *The New Advocate*, *12*(3), 259-276.

Ford, D. Y., Tyson, C. A., Howard, T. C., & Harris, J. J. (2000). Multicultural literature and gifted Black students: Promoting self-understanding, awareness, and pride. *Roeper Review*, *22*(4), 235-240.

Glenn-Paul, D. (1998). Bridging the cultural divide: Reflective dialogue about multicultural children's books. *The New Advocate*, *11*(3), 241-251.

Greene, B. M. (1995). Addressing race, class, and gender in Zora Neale Hurston's *Their Eyes Were Watching God: Strategies and reflections*. *English Education*, *27*(4), 268-276.

Gunther, M. A. (2000). Critical analysis of literature: Making the connection between reading and writing. *English Journal*, *89*(4), 85-88.

Harris, V. J. (1996). Continuing dilemmas, debates, and delights in multicultural literature. *The New Advocate*, *9*(2), 107-122.

Herz, S. K., & Gallo, D. (1996). *From Hinton to Hamlet: Building bridges between young adult literature and the classics*. Westport, CT.: Greenwood Press.

Hinton-Johnson, K. (2003). *Expanding the power of literature: African American literary theory and young adult literature*. Unpublished doctoral dissertation, The Ohio State University, Columbus.

Lasky, K. (1996). To Stingo with love: An author's perspective on writing outside one's culture. *The New Advocate, 9*(1), 1-7.

Martin, T. (1997). The care and feeding of the creative spirit: Teaching Alice Walker's "In Search of our Mothers' Gardens." *English Journal, 86*(8), 42-44.

Mayo, L. (2000). Making the connection: Reading and writing together. *English Journal, 89*(4), 74-77.

Menchaca, V. D. (2000). Providing a culturally relevant curriculum for Hispanic children. *Multicultural Education, 8*(3), 18-20.

Moore, J. N. (1997). *Interpreting young adult literature: Literary theory in the secondary classroom*. Portsmouth, NH: Boynton/Cook.

Nilsen, A. P., & Donelson, K. L. (1993). *Literature for today's young adults*. New York: HarperCollins College Publishers.

O'Malley, T. (1997). A ride down Mango Street. *English Journal, 86*(8), 35-37.

Page, M. L. (2004). Going beyond the book: A multicultural educator in the English language arts classroom. *Voices from the Middle, 12*(1), 8-15.

Pate, G. S. (1992). Reducing prejudice in society: The role of schools. In C. Diaz (Ed.), *Multicultural education for the 21st century* (pp. 166-178). Washington, D.C.: NEA.

Rhoades, G. (1991). Dealing with racism in the classroom. *Feminist Teacher, 6*(1), 34-36.

Roman, M. (1996). Nineteenth- and twentieth-century literature: Centering the margins.

In E. G. Friedman, W. K. Kolmar, C. B. Flint, & P. Rothenberg (Eds.), *Creating an inclusive college curriculum: A teaching sourcebook from the New Jersey project* (pp. 378-382). New York: Teachers College Press.

Rothenberg, P. (2000). Beyond the food court: goals and strategies for teaching multiculturalism. *Feminist Teacher, 13*(1), 61-73.

Scimone, A. J. (1999). At home with poetry: Constructing poetry anthologies in the high school classroom. *English Journal, 89*(2), 78-82.

Sleeter, C. E., & Grant, C. A. (1999). *Making choices for multicultural education: Five approaches to race, class, and gender*. New Jersey: Merrill.

Smith, V. (1997). Literary history. In W. L Andrews, F. S. Foster, & T. Harris (Eds.), *The Oxford companion to African American literature* (pp. 445-459). New York: Oxford University Press.

Soter, A. O. (1997). Reading literature of other cultures: Some issues in critical interpretation. In T. Rogers, & A. O. Soter (Eds.), *Reading across cultures: Teaching literature in a diverse society* (pp. 213-229). New York: Teachers College Press.

Soter, A. O. (1999). *Young adult literature and the new literary theories: Developing critical readers in middle school.* New York: Teachers College.

Spears-Bunton, L. A. (1990). Welcome to my house: African American and European American students' responses to Virginia Hamilton's "House of Dies Drear." *Journal of Negro Education, 59*(4), 566-576.

Taxel, J. (1992). The politics of children's literature: Reflections on multiculturalism, political correctness, and Christopher Columbus. In V. J. Harris (Ed.), *Teaching multicultural literature in grades k-8* (pp. 37-53). Norwood, MA: Christopher-Gordon Publishers, Inc.

Taxel, J. (1997). Multicultural literature and the politics of reaction. *Teachers College Record, 98*(3), 417-448.

Willis, A. I. (1997). Exploring multicultural literature as cultural production. In T. Rogers, & A. O. Soter (Eds.), *Reading across cultures: Teaching literature in a diverse society* (pp. 135-160). New York: Teachers College Press.

Chapter 2

Cultivating Young Adult Readers

Expanding Notions of Texts

In this day and time of books in print, on television, on MP3 players, and on CDs and audiotapes, it may be wise to begin with a view of what literature is. If you talk to most people about literature, the answer will be books. Certainly print books, magazines, graphic novels, and other types of print are included in a definition of literature. However, it is also important to mention e-books and i-books downloaded and listened to on MP3 players or computers. Books that have been adapted into movies or films are also an important part of our culture as are audiobooks and graphic novels.

The professional associations and societies that deal with literature also struggle with the sometimes-conflicting definitions of literature, but these associations present literary awards to all of these types of literature. By far, the two most prestigious awards for literature are the Newbery and Caldecott Awards, given to the best works in literature for children, presented by the Association for Library Service for Children (ALSC). Children, as defined by the ALSC, are from birth through age 14. Awards for young adult materials are presented by the Young Adult Library Services Association (YALSA), which defines young adults as those from age 12 to 18+. Hence, there will always be some overlap from both the ALSC and YALSA, both divisions of the American Library Association. Other national associations that provide reading and literature awards are the National Council of Teachers of English (NCTE), as well as other national associations in science and social studies. Even some states have awards for some types of literature (i.e., the Georgia Children's Book Award is given to picture books and middle grade novels).

Benefits of Awards

Awarding medals, prizes, and honors to books, videos, sound recordings, and their authors have many benefits. Using award-winning novels has not been proven to increase reading of those books, although it certainly helps book sales. It has, however, created an awareness of reading and of literature in our society, and it provides guidance for librarians and teachers in selecting quality literature in genres and formats in which they are unfamiliar or lack confidence. The ALSC and YALSA do not just present awards to noteworthy print books. Both organizations also prepare lists of notable sound recordings, films and videos, graphic novels, and other types of literature.

Another function of award lists is to make classroom teachers and librarians aware of materials that would otherwise slip our notice. Books published by university presses are usually not included in the lists generated by normal book distributors. If the American Association of University Publishers (AAUP) did not have a committee to identify books published by university presses of particular interest to public and secondary school libraries, we may never know about materials that are written by experts in the field about people and places of interest in the curriculum.

 Select Awards

Alex Award for books written for adults with young adult appeal
http://www.ala.org/Template.cfm?Section=bookmediaawards&template=/ContentManagement/ContentDisplay.cfm&ContentID=114076

Américas Book Award for Children's and Young Adult Literature that depicts Latin America, the Caribbean, or Latinos in the United States
http://www.uwm.edu/Dept/CLACS/outreach/americas.html

Asian Pacific American Award for Literature for children's and young adult literature that depicts Asian Pacific Americans
http://www.apalaweb.org/awards/awards.htm

Coretta Scott King Book Award for children's and young adult literature by and about African Americans
http://www.ala.org/ala/emiert/corettascottkingbookawards/corettascott.htm

Margaret A. Edwards Award for an author's complete contribution to young adult literature
http://www.ala.org/Template.cfm?Section=bookmediaawards&template=/ContentManagement/ContentDisplay.cfm&ContentID=119451

The Michael L. Printz Award for Excellence in Young Adult Literature
http://www.ala.org/Template.cfm?Section=bookmediaawards&template=/ContentManagement/ContentDisplay.cfm&ContentID=128605

Select Awards Continued

The Mildred L. Batchelder Award for a book translated into English
http://www.ala.org/ala/alsc/awardsscholarships/literaryawds/batchelderaward/
batchelderaward.htm

National Jewish Book Awards for children's and young adult literature about
Jewish themes
http://www.jewishbookcouncil.org/

Native Writers Circle of the Americas Award for lifetime contributions to
Native American literature
http://www.hanksville.org/storytellers/awards/lifetime.html

Pura Belpré Award for children's and young adult literature that depicts
Latino culture
http://www.ala.org/ala/alsc/awardsscholarships/literaryawds/belpremedal/
belprmedal.htm

Tomás Rivera Mexican American Children's Book Award for children's and
young adult literature that depicts Mexican Americans
http://www.education.txstate.edu/subpages/tomasrivera/

Young Adults' Choices Award is sponsored by the International Reading
Association for outstanding books chosen by young adults
http://www.reading.org/resources/tools/choices_young_adults.html

Separating Young Adult, Children's, and Adult Literature

The dividing line between young adult, children's, and adult books is not
easy to define. Robert Small, in 1992, reviewed the field of young adult literature and came up with some basic characteristics of what constitutes a YA
novel. He noted that YA novels tend to have a linear plot and be relatively
short, usually less than 200 pages. The time period covered by the novel is of
short duration, as little as a week and rarely more than one year. Major characters in the story are almost always young adults, with the protagonist
usually more mature and exhibiting a greater degree of wisdom or insightful-
ness than his or her peers, or may gain such maturity and wisdom over the
course of the novel. The story is told from the young adult protagonist's
point of view and adults are limited in helpfulness, or they could even be the
villains in the plot. Helpful adults, if any, are usually a teacher or coach.

Defining a Reader

In order to debate the degree to which young adults read, we turn to Donna
Shannon's (2003) characteristics of children, which can also be applied to
young adults, who read. She noted that READERs are children who read for

meaning, approach books and reading with enthusiasm, choose their own books, have an appreciation for different formats and genres, share and discuss what they read with others, and learn about themselves and their world through reading.

Most literacy researchers note that there is a path to creating readers. Strategies for creating readers include giving students time to read, encouraging book ownership, providing students with a wide variety of reading materials, and allowing students to choose which materials interests them. The power of adults like librarians and teachers in recommending books and other materials is also considered a powerful force in YA reading choices.

Cultivating Young Adult Readers

Some teachers and librarians may protest that their students do not read on a regular basis, but Stripling and Hughes-Hassell (2003) debated that premise. They note that young adults, in fact, do read quite a bit. They read magazines, newspapers, computer screens, text messages, and the crawl on television screens. They are not prone to read academic texts, but some of them read in-depth, think about what they read, and engage in conversations about their reading. The support that they get for their reading is not as strong as children's or adults, however. In libraries, a children's room might exist, but only rarely is there a teen room. In the big box (large, national) bookstores, the children's section again is delineated with murals, stuffed animals, child seating, and toys while the young adult or teen materials are usually one to two rows outside of the children's area, with no special invitations to teens to find their sections. Adults also enjoy comfortable reading and browsing areas in bookstores and libraries, but rarely do teens enjoy that privilege. Seldom are special programs, such as author visits, readings, or book discussion groups, held to celebrate teen readers. All of these programs are useful in an attempt to cultivate young adult readers.

It is true that some young adults use reading as a defense mechanism in order to withdraw from socialization, but that may be due to the lack of an outlet for YA avid readers to share in literature interactions, like book clubs and literature circles, with other avid readers or with adults in school. Still, young adult literature is alive and well, read by teens, debated and evaluated. It is unfortunately not given the same level of attention by adults as children's literature receives, nor is there an attempt to present this world of literature in the way that teens are most likely to be attracted to it.

Shelving By Genre

A recent conversation on library discussion lists regarding re-shelving of the middle school fiction collection by genre reflects this new attention to sparking YA interest in reading. At the early middle school age, a student is most likely to read by genre (i.e., animal books, or even more specifically, dog or horse books). Or they are hooked on romances, or mysteries, or adventure stories. Far from attempting to dissuade students from reading more of the same, some librarians are encouraging the reading habit of this age group by shelving and clearly labeling the genres together so that students can go to the scary stories section or the romance section and find all of the books that they want to read. In that way, reading and interacting with literature becomes a social act and can create a sense of ownership, since that small section of the library or classroom reading corner can feel like their own personal section.

Young Adult Literature for Below-Level Readers

Literature, including picture books, is useful to young adults reading below grade level. These students can benefit from the sparse text and illustrations that can help them feel successful as readers. The opposite of YA texts is probably the academic textbook, which can be dull reading, especially if the YA feels disconnected from its content. Reading literature in the secondary school classroom will enhance the student's ability to understand the textbook, and it will often include content that reinforces concepts mentioned in textbooks. (Vacca & Vacca, 2005) Literature can help motivate some students to learn about new topics. Moreover, literature can be used to make these topics, particularly those included in health, history, and science textbooks, seem relative when they are experienced by likeable characters in good literature. For example, while a textbook will delineate facts and issues around the beginning and continuation of slavery, books like Sharon Draper's *Copper Sun* (2006) or Gary Paulsen's *Nightjohn* (1993) can introduce students to rich characters whose lives were impacted by the institution of slavery in realistic and thought-provoking ways.

Similarly, in health class, the focus may be on infectious diseases, while in history the focus might be on Native Americans and the European discovery of North America. Jane Yolen's *Encounter* (1992) offers a rarely included perspective on European exploration while a book like Louise Erdrich's *The Birchbark House* (1999) treats both topics, providing insight into the way real people, particularly Native Americans, were affected by these events. Since textbooks cover a vast amount of material in a cursory way, literature can provide some depth to the topic (Vacca & Vacca, 2005).

Summary

Librarians and teachers can help create and cultivate young adult readers by making literature across the curriculum available and accessible to them in their libraries and classrooms. The children who enjoy booktalks, book readings, author visits, and other special programs and displays at bookstores and libraries have an enthusiasm for reading. Special sections in bookstores, trained professionals, and special events for young adults will continue to nurture this interest.

Works Cited

Draper, S. (2006). *Copper sun*. New York: Simon & Schuster.

Erdrich, L. (1999). *The birchbark house*. New York: Hyperion.

Paulsen, G. (1993). *Nightjohn*. New York: Delacorte.

Shannon, D. M. (2003). Literacy learning in the elementary school: Implications for school library media specialists. In B. K. Stripling, & S. Hughes-Hassell (Eds.), *Curriculum connections through the library* (pp. 67-85). Westport, CT: Libraries Unlimited.

Small, R. C. (Spring 1992). The literary value of the young adult novel. *Journal of Youth Services in Libraries*, 277-285.

Vacca, R. T., & Vacca, J. A. (2005). *Content area reading: Literacy and learning across the curriculum*. Boston: Pearson.

Yolen, J. (1992). *Encounter*. San Diego, CA: Harcourt Brace.

Chapter 3

Classroom Teachers/ School Library Media Team

B oth the classroom teacher and the school library media specialist share one of the strongest barriers to a true student-centered and individualized approach to implementing an integrated multicultural individualized education program. Ironically, the barrier can also be one of the easiest to overcome if the teacher and school library media specialist collaborates. That barrier is time. The classroom teacher stares at the class of 25 individual students and sighs over the difficulty of planning strategies around multicultural resources with whole-class instruction. The school library media specialist looks over the school's collection of multicultural resources and sighs over the difficulty of getting them into the hands of the students. Collaboration is the answer.

Special educators know the value of collaborative teaching as a way to include their students in mainstream instruction. Marilyn Friend and Lynne Cook (1993), when writing about co-teaching, list four types of collaborative-teaching pertinent to librarian-teacher collaboration. These are assistive, parallel, alternative, and team teaching. These types of teaching are not scaffolded, but rather are chosen according to the learning and teaching needs.

- The teacher or the librarian may take the primary role in instruction (assistive teaching).
- They may divide the class and conduct the same activity in small groups (parallel teaching).
- They may conduct a different activity according to the needs of each group (alternative teaching).

- They might also work together to have joint instructional roles in the delivery of instruction (team teaching).

The learning needs of the students translated into instruction should determine the types of co-teaching between the librarian and classroom teacher.

The use of taxonomies to measure and scale teacher-school librarian collaboration was popularized by David Loertscher's *Taxonomies of the School Library Media Program* (2000). In those taxonomies, Loertscher outlined a program of growing cooperation and collaboration. In this chapter, we will look at those taxonomies applied to multicultural strategies.

Level 1 – No Involvement

In this scenario, the classroom teacher develops and implements multicultural strategies that are classroom-contained. The resources used are those in the teacher's classroom or are available through Web sites and databases. The instruction may be inspired, creative, well planned and well taught but is based on time allowed and materials at hand.

The school library media specialist also works alone. Displays for Black History Month or Women's Studies may be inspired, creative, well planned and well taught, but they are based on the premise that students will enter the library to use them on their own time and of their own volition.

Level 2 – Smoothly Operating Information Infrastructure

At this level, some thought is given to the world outside of the individual worlds of classroom and library. The classroom teacher makes an attempt to gather more resources, perhaps to augment the classroom collection. The teacher may even enter the library to check the collection for materials to assign for parallel reading for a subject area, or to ensure that the library has adequate resources for an assignment on women scientists and mathematicians. At this level, the organization of the library and the efficiency of the circulation process are all that are required to ensure the success of this level of the taxonomy.

The school library media specialist also reaches outside of the library castle for this level of involvement. He or she may make a list of new resources or even prepare a bibliography of resources on specific subjects. However, the lack of direct communication hurts the efficiency of the smooth operation of the library warehouse. The materials that the school library media specialist acquires and publicizes may or may not be timely or appropriate to the subject, grade level, or instructional methodologies of the classroom teacher. In the best of worlds, the classroom teacher may bring the list back to the library to check out the resources, but this is more of a coincidence than a consequence.

Level 3 – Individual Reference Assistance

At this level, the classroom teacher and the school library media specialist act as intermediaries between their boundaries and the student. A classroom teacher may assign parallel reading or an assignment that requires research skills. The student approaches the teacher for individual confirmation of the assignment, and then heads to the library for assistance in finding materials. In another scenario, the teacher may give a broader assignment, such as reading a novel that presents a multicultural view of history. In this scenario, the student may check out a book, or several books, and present it to the teacher for approval and appropriate "fit" for the assignment.

Note that there is little to no direct communication between the school librarian and the classroom teacher. Each of them stands firm at the doorway to their own separate turf, allowing the student to traverse the ground in-between.

Level 4 – Spontaneous Interaction and Gathering

This level of the taxonomy moves from the library and classroom as separate warehouses of learning to some degree of interaction. Notes and e-mails can be used to pass information between the library and the classroom. At this level, the classroom teacher requests materials on specific topics. The school librarian gathers the materials and allows the classroom teacher to take them and display them, or even have the classroom teacher responsible for checking them out to students. The materials are chosen only on the criteria of the subject or topic. How the materials will be used or any participation by the school librarian in teaching strategies does not occur at this level.

Level 5 – Cursory Planning

Hand-in-hand with spontaneous gathering in Level 4 is the type of planning that occurs through e-mails or brief hallway meetings. At this level, conversations occur about types of strategies. Sentences that begin "I'm thinking about…" or "Have you tried…?" allow the school library media specialist and classroom teacher to discuss how materials can be used in the instructional process. At this level, however, the planning is truly cursory, and is limited to one or two brief e-mails or conversations only minutes in length. Still, this level may set the stage for more in-depth collaboration in the future.

Level 6 – Planned Gathering

In Level 4, the school librarian gathers materials upon request of the classroom teacher. However, at this level, the communication is limited to subject or topic, yet communication reaches a deeper level. The school library media specialist and classroom teacher discuss not only the subject or topic of the materials to be gathered but also how the materials will be used. The classroom teacher may still develop the assignment, implement the instruction, and assess student learning, but the school librarian is informed of what the assignment is and the general purpose of the teaching unit. The school librarian is better able to gather appropriate materials in a wide range of formats. As a result, the classroom teacher receives materials better suited to the purpose of the unit.

Level 7 – Evangelistic Outreach/Advocacy

At this level, the classroom teacher and school library media specialist actively sees the value of working together, and they share that information with others. The school library media specialist is enthusiastic and proactive with suggesting resources for the classroom teacher and may make a concerted effort to suggest materials, teaching strategies, or assessment tips. The classroom teacher is receptive and appreciative of the resources and suggestions. Prior planning for instructional activities is still at a minimum at this level, but there is a shared concept of instruction, and the classroom teacher may slowly come to rely on resources from the library to augment the class text.

For multicultural integration and collaboration at this stage, most units have some outside materials that can be used. The classroom teacher has shared information about the subjects to be taught and concepts to be covered in the future. The school library media specialist understands the type of resources that would be most helpful. Interaction between the school library media specialist and the students and teachers happens frequently, and the school library media specialist is aware of assignments before the students appear in the library. Co-teaching happens frequently, and the students and teacher are frequent visitors in the library. Occasionally, the school librarian will co-teach in the classroom.

Level 8 – Implementation of the Four Major Programmatic Elements of the LMC Program

The four major programmatic elements of the school library program are as follows:

- Collaborative teaching of information skills
- Reading encouragement
- Using technology to locate, access, and use information
- Information literacy skills

At this level, the interaction between the classroom teacher and school library media specialist covers all four of these elements. True collaboration means co-planning of instruction, co-teaching the unit, and co-assessment of student progress. Although collaboration does not occur constantly, it will occur frequently. Some part of the continuum of collaboration (cooperation, coordination, and collaboration) is present in almost every unit, even if it is just the provision of a small number of resources for the teacher to use in the classroom.

In the programmatic element of reading encouragement, the school library media specialist actively tries to provoke student interest in free voluntary reading. Displays in the library coordinate with classroom subjects, and it is not unusual for displays of materials to be in the classroom as well. Parallel reading is either required for classroom units or offered as extra credit. Reading, even the reading of fiction, is seen as an important way to deliver content, and as a way to make the curricular subject come alive to students.

Learning is constantly enhanced through technology. Web resources, use of audiovisual materials, and other ways to use technology in the teaching and learning process is explored and implemented whenever possible. The school library media specialist and classroom teacher work together to infuse technology in both the delivery of instruction and in student projects for research. By partnering, the effect of having two teachers working with hands-on projects streamlines the time needed for instruction and enhances the student products.

All of the above are enhanced by the skills of information literacy instruction. The students are gaining skill and confidence by the knowledge that information on topics covered in class is available in other formats. Students are free to explore concepts on their own and may actively seek to use their own initiative to look for more information or to browse current magazines of information. Students are portrayed as information literate in casual conversation between teachers and in official communications to the school community.

Level 9 – The Mature LMC Program

The type of interaction described in Level 8 benefits both the classroom teacher and the school library media specialist. The barrier of time that prevented each from moving outside their own individual worlds has disappeared, as both the casual and formal planning and interaction stages happen on a regular basis and are integrated into the school day. In this level of the taxonomy, however, the interaction between this one teacher and the school library media specialist has now spread to the entire school.

Success has a ripple effect in school. Soon other teachers in the department noticed that there was more creative instruction happening, that the students were more engaged, and that even test scores may have been rising because the variety of materials used ensured a higher level of student learning. Inquiries may have been made into how this was accomplished, and fingers pointed to the library as a resource for materials and for material assistance.

Students may have asked teachers in other departments why they could not do the activities that they did elsewhere, and their teachers may have investigated exactly what was going on down the hall.

In a highly collaborative school, the entire faculty works with each other to ensure that all available resources are used appropriately for the purpose of enhancing student learning. A natural consequence of this high level of collaboration means that the classroom teachers and the school librarians work together to ensure that both all students and each student are learning. That all students learn is a caveat of many educational programs. It is easy, however, to overlook that in order for all students to learn, each student has to learn as well. Finding the right resources and the right type of learning environment for that to happen is enhanced by adding the library as a learning laboratory to the classroom structure.

Level 10 – Curriculum Development

In Level 10, the focus moves away from the classroom. At the curriculum development level, integration of a multicultural approach to student learning is written into the standards, the curriculum, the learning activities, the resources, and the assessments.

Reprinted here with permission from Dr. David V. Loertscher

Summary

In the taxonomic process, integration of a multicultural approach to learning moves from no involvement to the classroom level, then to the school level, and then finally to the district level.

Works Cited

Friend, M., & Cook, L. (1993). *Integrations*. White Plains, NY: Longmans.
Loertscher, D. V. (2000). *Taxonomies of the school library media program* (2nd ed.). San Jose, CA: Hi Willow.

Chapter 4

Race and Ethnicity

R ace and ethnicity are slippery, debatable, and confusing terms. We see race as a social construction largely based on an individual's visible physical features such as skin color and hair texture. Often people use the terms racial and ethnic interchangeably when referring to people who are considered Asian, black, white, and Native American. Manning and Baruth (1996) define ethnicity as, "people's national origin, religion, and/or race" (p. 41). Ibieta and Orvell (1996) suggest that the current meaning of ethnic is "peculiar to a race or nation…an ethnic is an *other* and thus ethnicity is something that is defined in terms of cultural difference…what is not 'us' is ethnic" (p. 2).

Some of the books in this chapter focus on topics that explore (bi)racial/ethnic identity development and racial conflict while others celebrate racial and ethnic difference, cross-racial relationships, and immigration experiences.

Integrating Multicultural Texts

Code Talker: A Novel About the Navajo Marines of World War Two by Joseph Bruchac, Dial, 2005

Ned Begay tells his grandchildren about his life, beginning with his enrollment at Rehobeth Mission School, a boarding school, when he was six and his desire to enlist in the United States Marine Corp during World War II. The faculty and staff of the mission school sought to fully acculturate Ned and his schoolmates, changing their names to English names, cutting their hair, selling their Turquoise jewelry and other belongings, and forbidding them to speak their language. When the children resisted, they were punished severely, yet, many of them like Ned found ways to cling to their native language. When Ned turned 15, he learned that the military had suddenly found use for Navajo men and their language. They began to recruit men between the ages of 17 and 35 to participate in a secret effort to help win the war. Though Ned is too young to enlist, his parents allow him to do so when he is 16. The first group of 29 Navajo Marines created an unbreakable code based on the Navajo language that was used to communicate secretly. Ned describes his contribution as a code talker in the fight against Japan.

Suggestions for Classroom Use

1. Create a K-W-L chart. Under K- write down everything you know about Navajo code talkers during World War II. In the column headed W-, write down what you want to know about Navajo code talkers. In the column headed L-, write down what you learn about Navajo code talkers after reading Bruchac's novel.

2. View the movie *Windtalkers* directed by John Woo. Discuss the cinematic aspects (angle shots, sound track, casting, sets, and so forth.) of the film.

3. After viewing the movie, read *Windtalkers: The Making of the John Woo Film About the Navajo Code Talkers of World War II* edited by Antonia Felix, and study the stills taken from the film and the historic photographs from the U.S. Marines and the National Archives.

4. Read other books about Navajo Code Talkers: *Navajo Code Talkers* by Nathan Aaseng's, *Warriors: Navajo Code Talkers* by Kenji Kawano, and *Unsung Heroes of World War II: The Story of the Navajo Code Talkers* by Deanne Durrett. Record details about the code's origins and how it was used during World War II.

 Read Alike

If you like *Moccasin Thunder: American Indian Stories for Today* (HarperCollins, 2005), edited by Lori M. Carlson, try *Rising Voices: Writings of Young Native Americans* (Simon & Schuster, 1992) edited by Arlene Hirschfelder and Beverly R. Singer.

5. Research articles in full-text newspapers and magazine databases to find information about the Congressional Medal of Honor ceremony for the living code talkers held in 2001.

6. Chart Begay's travels while serving during World War II.

7. Compare what you learn about World War II in the novel with information your history textbook includes about it.

Beacon Hill Boys by Ken Mochizuki, Scholastic, 2002

Dan Inagaki, a junior at Herbert Hoover High School, lives in Beacon Hill, a Seattle neighborhood, during the early 1970s. In search of cultural identity, he longs to learn more about his family's past, but they refuse to talk about it, especially the family's stay in the internment camps of World War II. At school Dan wants the Asian students to be politically active, yet he notices that there is strong interest in becoming acculturated rather than highlighting or celebrating difference. Dan's own brother symbolizes this, and according to his parents, serves as the perfect role model for Dan. With his friends—Jerry Ito, Eddie Kanagae, and Frank Ishimoto—at his side, Dan sets out to try to change his world.

Suggestions for Classroom Use

1. Explain why Dan is accused of being an agitator. Is he an agitator? Why or why not?

2. Create a chart with three columns headed Stereotypes, Cultural Expectations, and Self-Perceptions. In the column labeled Stereotypes, write down preconceived notions characters have about various cultural groups. In the column labeled Cultural Expectations, write down ideas about Japanese culture that Dan and his friends believe are ascribed to their culture by Nisei (his parent's generation). In the column labeled, Self-Perceptions write down ideas about Japanese culture that Dan and his friends seem to invest in.

3. Write a letter to Dan from Brad explaining his feelings about his heritage and identity as a Japanese American.

4. Describe Dan's grandmother and her function in the novel.

5. The author includes a discography at the end of the book. What role does music play in the novel?

6. Do research to learn what life was like in the United States during the 1970s. For example, what presidents were in office, what social movements were active, what sparked the Vietnam War, and so on?

Cuba 15 by Nancy Osa, Random House, 2003

Fifteen-year-old Violet Paz is stunned when her grandmother urges her to have a quinceañera, a coming-of-age celebration for Latina young women. Though Violet's father is Cuban, she knows very little about Cuban customs and traditions. Her father, because of bitter feelings about Fidel Castro and Communism, refuses to discuss his heritage with her or her brother Mark.

     Planning for the quince celebration sparks Violet's interest in her heritage and she begins to ask questions of her family. When her parents offer little help, she reaches out to her Aunt Luz, researches Cuba for her Spanish class, attends a peace rally, and looks closely at her extended family.

Suggestions for Classroom Use

1. Create a picture book of facts about Cuba to help Violet learn more about her Cuban heritage.

2. Write a diary entry as Dad describing why he does not want to discuss his Cuban culture with Violet and Mark.

3. Violet does not mention very much about her Polish heritage. Research and write a short paper about why people from Poland might have immigrated to the United States.

4. Research the conditions in Cuba that possibly led to Abuelo and Abuela's immigration to the United States.

5. Violet says, "Spanish was currency. Currency I didn't have." What does this mean and what evidence is there in the text to support Violet's claim?

Read Alike

If you like *The Heart of a Chief* (Dial, 1998) by Joseph Bruchac, try *Who Will Tell My Brother?* (Hyperion, 2002) by Marlene Carvell.

6. Use in a language unit: Locate the Spanish words and phrases in the book and create an English/Spanish glossary.

7. Read *Quinceañera Means Sweet 15* by Veronica Chambers and *Quinceañera: Celebrating Fifteen* by Elizabeth King. Compare the details given about the celebration across the three books.

In the Research — Mentors and Monsters

Author of *Cuba 15* (Delacorte, 2003), Nancy Osa, describes how she stumbled upon the story idea that led to her successful first novel for young adults. The article also includes excerpts from her journal describing her thoughts about how her life might have been different had her family been able to live both in the United States and Cuba. Excerpts from her personal letters describe her longing to reach out to relatives in Cuba from the suburbs of Chicago. She also discusses how she sought out mentors, such as young adult author, Virginia Euwer Wolff and writer, Alma Flor Ada, who encouraged her while she worked on the novel. The article announces her receipt of the 19th Delacorte Press Prize for *Cuba 15*.

Osa, N. (2003). Mentors and monsters. *The Alan Review, 30*(2), 13-15.

Select Awards & Honors
Pura Belpré Honor Book
An ALA Notable Book
An ALA Best Book for Young Adults
A *Booklist* Top Ten Youth First Novels

Home of the Brave by Allen Say, Houghton Mifflin, 2002

A male protagonist has an accident while kayaking and dreams of Japanese children wearing nametags who were once inhabitants of an internment camp during World War II. As the protagonist follows the children around the camp, he wanders into a house and finds a nametag with his name on it.

Suggestions for Classroom Use

1. Write a short paper about what life was like for some Japanese people during World War II prior to being interned and after the internment.

2. In preparation for a debate, develop arguments based on United States' views concerning reasons for internment camps and Japanese citizens' thoughts about being interned.

3. Before reading the text, make predictions about what the text will be about. Begin with the cover and examine the pictures on each page before reading the text. Write a journal entry recording the story the pictures alone seem to tell. Share your interpretation in small groups.

 Read Alike

If you like *American Dragons: Twenty-Five Asian American Voices* (HarperCollins, 1993) edited by Laurence Yep, try Jacqueline Woodson's *A Way Out of No Way: Writings About Growing Up Black in America* (Henry Holt, 1996).

4. Imagine a dialogue between the protagonist and his mother in which she tells him about her experiences in an internment camp.

5. What was life like for children in the internment camps? What was life like for children on Indian reservations during the 1940s? During contemporary times?

Montana, 1948 by Larry Watson, Milkweed, 1993

David Hayden, a teacher, reflects on the events that sparked family turmoil in 1948 when he was 12 years old. David, the son and grandson of sheriffs in the western plains fictional town of Bentrock, and the rest of the family learn that Uncle Frank, the town doctor, is molesting Native American women. When the Hayden's housekeeper, Marie Little Soldier, a Sioux Indian, becomes ill, she becomes terrified when there is talk of having Uncle Frank examine her. David's father must arrest his own brother for violating women in the area and for possibly murdering Marie. The story has a mysterious tone as messages about justice, racism, love, and family abound.

Suggestions for Classroom Use

1. Quickwrite/Freewrite: Define loyalty and justice. How do these concepts relate to the novel?

2. Write a book review of *Montana, 1948.*

3. Write at least one paragraph describing how Marie Little Soldier was portrayed.

4. Write at least one paragraph describing how David feels about Uncle Frank. Marie Little Soldier?

5. Write an obituary for Marie Little Soldier and Uncle Frank.

6. Research to find out about the Native American tribes that lived in Montana in the 1940s.

Select Awards & Honors
1993 Milkweed National Fiction Prize

Additional Titles

Bless Me, Ultima by Rudolfo Anaya, Tonatiuh International, 1972

Set in New Mexico during World War II, the novel focuses on the maturation process of Antonio Márez. Confused by the conflicting views of his parents and larger society, Antonio has to make sense of his surroundings. His experiences with Ultima, one of the last curanderas, or healers, have a lasting impact on his journey toward maturity.

American Eyes: New Asian-American Short Stories for Young Adults edited by Lori Marie Carlson, Henry Holt & Company, 1994

Each of the eight stories, and two novel excerpts, in this collection explore concepts of home, identity, and culture within the works of Asian American writers as diverse as Cynthia Kadohata, Fae Myenne Ng, and Marie G. Lee, among others. Kadohata's introduction raises questions about the place of race and culture within literature.

Moccasin Thunder: American Indian Stories for Today edited by Lori Marie Carlson, HarperCollins, 2005

Ten stories focus on the experiences of contemporary Native American youth who realize poverty, friendship, history, tradition, and love. Some of the well-known authors in this collection include Joy Harjo, Sherman Alexie, and Joseph Bruchac.

Yellow Raft in Blue Water by Michael Dorris, Henry Holt & Company, 1987

Narrated by three different women: 15-year-old Rayona Taylor, her mother, Christine, and Christine's "mother," Aunt Ida. Rayona, daughter of a Native American mother and an African American father, feels unsure of her identity. Treated like an outsider because of her mixed heritage, Rayona finds life on the reservation difficult. Like her mother and Aunt Ida before her, she eventually runs away in search of a new direction for her life.

Love Medicine by Louise Erdrich, Holt, 1984

When June Kashpaw, a prostitute, freezes to death, her family comes together to share stories about her and to reveal something of themselves. The multiple narrators include members from several families: the Nanapushes, the Kashpaws, the Pilagers, the Lazarres, and the Morrisseys.

The Known World by Edward P. Jones, Amistad, 2003

Henry Townsend, a farmer, bootmaker, and ex-slave, with the help of his former master, William Robbins, becomes a slave owner himself. After his death, his widow, Caldonia, is left to take charge of the Townsend plantation, home to over thirty slaves, but she encounters several problems that threaten the survival of the plantation.

The Woman Warrior: Memoirs of a Girlhood Among Ghosts by Maxine Hong Kingston, Knopf, 1976

Set in China and California, autobiography, fiction, and mythology collide relating stories from Kingston's family and informants in the community where she grew up. At the heart of the book is an examination of Chinese culture and American acculturation.

Native Speaker by Chang-Rae Lee, Riverhead, 1995

Narrator Henry Park lives in New York City and works as an undercover agent. Dealing with difficulties in his marriage, the death of his son, and a new assignment that requires him to spy on John Kwang, a Korean American politician with hopes of running for mayor of New York, are only a few of the challenges Henry faces.

House Made of Dawn by N. Scott Momaday, Harper, 1968

During his youth, Abel, a Pueblo Indian and World War II veteran, learned about his cultural history from Francisco, his grandfather. As an adult, Abel is consumed with notions of double consciousness as he finds it difficult to reconcile traditional cultural heritage and spiritual beliefs with twentieth century sensibilities.

When the Emperor Was Divine by Julie Otsuka, Knopf, 2002

This novel focuses on the three-year period of a nameless family's experiences in an internment camp in the desert during World War II. The poetic language and vivid description conveys the family's plight beginning the moment they receive notice that they will be interned.

Mixed: An Anthology of Short Fiction on the Multiracial Experience edited by Chandra Prasad, W.W. Norton, 2006

This collection contains 18 stories about biracial characters written by biracial authors. The explicit references to sex, characters in adult situations, and the frequent use of profanity might make this book more appropriate for mature readers.

Ceremony by Leslie Marmon Silko, Viking, 1977

Tayo, a young Native American, enlists in the military and travels to the Philippines during World War II. When he returns to the Laguna Pueblo reservation, he finds it difficult to adjust.

A Suitcase of Seaweed and Other Poems by Janet S. Wong, Simon & Schuster, 1996

Wong divides this book of free verse poetry into three sections, Korean, Chinese, and American, representative of her own cultural affiliations. There are poems about various topics such as food, heritage, and hair.

American Dragons: Twenty-Five Asian American Voices edited by Laurence Yep, HarperCollins, 1993

Divided into six sections headed "Identity," "In the Shadow of Giants," "The Wise Child," "World War Two," "Love," and "Guides," this collection includes poems, stories, and excerpts from novels and plays by some of today's leading Asian American writers, including Maxine Hong Kingston and Jeanne Wakatsuki Houston. Six main cultural groups are featured: Tibetan, Vietnamese, Chinese, Korean, Japanese, and Thai.

Dragonwings by Laurence Yep, HarperCollins, 1975

Moon Shadow travels from China to live with his father in San Francisco, California where they endure injustice and poverty. Though they suffer injustices and endure hard labor, they never abandon the father's dream of becoming a kite-builder.

Works Cited

Ibieta, G., & Orvell, M. (1996). *Inventing America*. NY: St. Martin's Press.

Manning, M. L., & Baruth, L. G. (1996). *Multicultural education of children and adolescents* (2nd ed.). Boston, MA: Allyn & Bacon.

Osa, N. (2003). Mentors and monsters. *The Alan Review, 30*(2), 13-15.

Chapter *5*

Gender and Sexuality

D uring the last 30 years multicultural literature has been used in classrooms across the country to spark conversations about gender issues. Students and teachers have looked closely at literature that includes progressive depictions of gender roles while also reading against, or deconstructing, those books that contain questionable portrayals of male and female roles. More recently, books have also been used to discuss concerns facing gay and lesbian youth. Looking deeply at the diversity of family units, the curiosity of questioning youth, and the causes of homophobia has encouraged students and teachers to examine their thoughts, feelings, and beliefs about sexuality. Many teachers and researchers feel it is important for adults to have conversations with young people about gender stereotypes, gender inequity, homosexuality, heterosexism, and homophobia while hoping that these conversations will emphasize the students' own power to challenge and, perhaps, change bias in its numerous forms.

While all of the books mentioned in this chapter can be used to further these conversations, some of the titles focus specifically on the struggles young girls and boys face while growing up in our society, a society that often shows conflicting images concerning what it means to be male and female. The girls and boys depicted in many of these books struggle with whether they should deny their own ambitions and interests in order to take on roles prescribed by societal expectations. Thus, many of the books also purposely challenge sexual stereotyping by portraying brave, smart, female protagonists, as well as non-stereotypical depictions of boys. Other books depict characters who are exploring the possibility of being lesbian or gay, who actually are lesbian or gay, as well as those who feel discriminated against because of their sexuality.

Multicultural Resources

Online Resources

www.guysread.com

Other Resources

Life Is Tough: Guys, Growing Up, and Young Adult Literature
by Rachelle Lasky Bilz
Scarecrow Press, 2004

The Heart Has Its Reasons: Young Adult Literature with Gay/Lesbian/Queer Content, 1969-2004
by Michael Cart and Christine A. Jenkins
Rowman & Littlefield, 2006

Lesbian and Gay Voices: An Annotated Bibliography and Guide to Literature for Children and Young Adults
by Frances Ann Day
Greenwood, 2000

"Teen Chick Lit"
by Christine Meloni
Library Media Connection, 25(2), October 2006, p. 16-19

Integrating Multicultural Texts

Real Women Have Curves, 2002, Screenplay by George Lavoo and Josefina Lopez
Directed by Patricia Cardoso, HBO Films, Rating: PG 13

Eighteen-year-old Ana decides she wants to pursue a college degree rather than work in her sister's dress factory or get married. Despite her mother's insistence that she develop into a respectable, traditional Latina, Ana challenges the traditional role of women.

Suggestions for Classroom Use

1. What's the significance of the title? What does it mean? Create two alternative titles and explain your choices.

2. Explain why Ana feels torn between two worlds, two cultures.

3. Explain why Estella accepts only $18.00 for the dresses she sells to manufacturers when she knows department stores will sell them for much more.

4. Explain why Ana's parents are opposed to her going to college.

5. Describe how the roles of men and women are different in Ana's family.

6. Ana's mother feels it is important for her to develop into a woman. What does this entail?

7. Many women feel pressured to adhere to a beauty aesthetic that seems unobtainable. Describe how this is portrayed in the movie.

8. Develop a conversation between Ana and her mother after she has completed her freshman year of college.

Select Awards & Honors

Audience Award at Sundance Film Festival 2002

Rainbow Boys by Alex Sanchez, Simon & Schuster, 2001

The first in a series of books that include *Rainbow High* and *Rainbow Road*, this novel captures the lives of three young men—Jason Carrillo, Kyle Meeks, and Nelson Glassman—as they develop acceptance of their own sexuality.

Suggestions for Classroom Use

1. Create a character sketch of one of the three main characters. What does he look like? What are his hobbies and interests? What type of character is he? How does he handle conflict?

2. Using a Venn diagram, compare and contrast the three main characters. How are they alike? How are they different?

3. Does your school have a Gay/Straight Alliance? If your school doesn't have a Gay/Straight Alliance, create a survey to find out if students are interested in establishing one. If your school does have a Gay/Straight Alliance, create a survey that will help you find out about the services it provides, the number of members involved, and the general history of your school's chapter.

4. Using a research source, find out more about Parents, Families and Friends of Lesbians and Gays (PFLAG) and some of the other organizations the author lists at the back of the book. Why do you think the author put this information in the book?

5. Visit the Centers for Disease Control and Prevention's Web site, <www.cdc.gov>, to learn more about HIV/AIDS, especially about how it is transmitted.

6. Visit <www.pflag.org> and find out if there is a chapter in your area.

7. Define homophobia. How is its impact illustrated in the book?

Shortly after the publication of his first book for young adults, Alex Sanchez talked to Toby Emert about the book's inception, popularity, and importance as one of few books available in 2001 that openly discusses gay males, HIV/AIDS, homophobia, gay/straight alliances, and other support organizations for GLBTQ (gay, lesbian, bisexual, transgender, or questioning) teens.

Emert, T. (2002). An interview with Alex Sanchez, author of *Rainbow Boys*. *The Alan Review* 29(3), 12-14.

True Believer by Virginia Euwer Wolff, Atheneum, 2001

In this sequel to *Make Lemonade*, LaVaughn struggles with questions about sexuality, abstinence, and first love. Through it all, she never lets go of her desire to go to college.

Suggestions for Classroom Use

1. Read *Make Lemonade*, the companion to *True Believer*. How has LaVaughn changed? How does the author show that the LaVaughn depicted in *True Believer* is growing up?

   - Use the REAP strategy (Vacca & Vacca, 2005) while reading this novel. **R**ead the text; **E**ncode the text by summarizing the plot; **A**nnotate the text by writing down its theme; and **P**onder the text by writing about how you felt while reading and discussing your thoughts with classmates.

Read Alike

If you like *Keeping You a Secret* (Little, Brown, Co., 2003) by Julie Anne Peters, try Jacqueline Woodson's *The House You Pass on the Way* (Delacorte, 1997).

2. Create a double-entry journal while reading this book. On one side of a sheet of paper jot down the main issues that the text mentions about gender. On the other side, write down your thoughts and feelings about these issues.

3. Be a character detective. Record clues (i.e., How does he act and what does he say?) that help you describe Jody's character.

4. What obstacles might hinder LaVaughn from accomplishing her goals?

From the Notebooks of Melanin Sun by Jacqueline Woodson, Scholastic, 1995

Melanin Sun records conflicting thoughts about his mother's relationship with a white woman in his journal. He is also trying to make sense of his own budding sexuality.

Suggestions for Classroom Use

1. Before reading *From the Notebooks of Melanin Sun*, write briefly about a time when you learned something about a family member, particularly a parent, that you did not know before. How did you feel when you found this information out? Did this new information change how you felt about the person?

2. Suppose Melanin's mother also kept a journal. Write an entry from her perspective.

3. Predict how Melanin's thoughts, attitude, and feelings might change after he gets to know Kristin.

4. Highlight passages that indicate Melanin's opinions about race. What does Melanin seem to believe about white people?

5. Using the QAR (Question, Answer, Relationship) strategy (Vacca & Vacca, 2005), create three types of questions to test your classmates' understanding of the text:

   a. Right There Questions. The answers to these questions can be found in the book.

   Ex. Why is Melanin Sun angry with his mother?

   b. Think and Search Questions. The answers to these questions can be found in the book, but they are not often explicitly stated and the complete answer is usually found in more than one place in the text.

   Ex. How does Melanin Sun change by the end of the novel?

   c. On Your Own Questions. The answers to these questions can be found in the reader's own thoughts and prior knowledge.

   Ex. Have you ever had to accept a decision someone made that affected you though you didn't agree with it?

In the Reseach   **Making It Real**

The authors describe the literacy practices of TEEN (Teens Educating in the Environment Needed for Teens), a group of teenage girls from the Bronx in Jennifer Tendero's class who wanted to study realistic issues, issues relative to their own lives. The girls were concerned about sexual experimentation, teenage pregnancy, and teen motherhood, so they read fiction and nonfiction and interviewed teen mothers in search of answers to some of their questions. After reading Sandra Cisneros' *The House on Mango Street*, students wrote about growing up in their neighborhoods in New York. Students also looked at ways other novels like *The Woman Warrior: Memoirs of a Girlhood Among Ghosts* (Vintage, 1976), *Walk Two Moons* (HarperCollins, 1994), and *Like Sisters on the Homefront* (Lodestar, 1995) connected with their lives.

Schaafsma, D., Tendero, A., & Tendero, J. (1999). Making it real: Girls' stories, social change, and moral struggle. *English Journal, 88*(5), 28-36.

Additional Titles

On Her Way: Stories and Poems About Growing Up Girl edited by Sandy Asher, Penguin, 2004

Edwidge Danticat, Marion Dane Bauer, Angela Johnson, and Linda Sue Park are among the more than 15 authors who contributed stories and poems to this collection. Many of the characters break gender "rules," search for freedom, and dare to be different all while growing up to become women.

Am I Blue?: Coming Out from the Silence edited by Marion Dane Bauer, HarperCollins, 1994

Sixteen stories by famous young adult writers focus on growing up gay and lesbian. Some of the stories make the injustice of homophobia and heterosexism visible to readers.

Love and Sex: Ten Stories of Truth edited by Michael Cart, Simon & Schuster, 2001

Well-known authors such as Laurie Halse Anderson, Chris Lynch, and Angela Johnson contribute stories to this collection that will satisfy any teen's curiosity about sex. The collection deals with various sex-related topics, from virginity to a teenaged boy's first crush on a boy.

Party Girl by Lynne Ewing, Alfred Knopf, 1998

Best friends Ana and Kata, Outrageous Chaos, sneak out late at night to participate in a dance competition in an abandoned warehouse. At 14, Ana gets pregnant with hopes of getting out of the gang life, but she is killed by an enemy gang member while Kata has to decide if she's going to avenge Ana's death.

Things I Have to Tell You: Poems and Writing by Teenage Girls edited by Betsy Franco, photographs by Nina Nickles, Candlewick, 2001

This book, similar to its companion, *You Hear Me?: Poems and Writing by Teenage Boys* (Candlewick, 2000), features poems, stories, and essays written by teenage girls that are accompanied by black and white photographs of young women from different cultures. The girls raise issues about a number of topics, including sexuality, beauty aesthetics, and social issues.

Read Alike

If you like Jon Scieszka's *Guys Write for Guys Read* (Viking, 2005), try *Dude! Stories and Stuff for Boys* (Penguin, 2006) edited by Sandy Asher and David L.

Annie on My Mind by Nancy Garden, Farrar, Straus and Giroux, 1982

This classic describes the budding relationship between Liza and Annie during their high school years. Told in retrospect, the novel describes the girls' maturity and self-discovery during an important period of their lives.

Deliver Us from Evie by M.E. Kerr, HarperCollins, 1994

Sixteen-year-old Parr Burrman describes his parents and his farm community's reaction to his non-conventional older sister Evie. It is Evie's relationship with Patsy Duff, the daughter of a man who owns most of their town, Duffton, Missouri, however, that brings about the greatest level of conflict for the family.

Boy Meets Boy by David Levithan, Random House, 2003

Set in an idealistic society where diversity is often celebrated, protagonist Paul develops an interest in Noah after meeting him at a bookstore. While his friendship develops with Noah, his friendship with his close friend Tony, a gay young man living with Christian parents, seems to be in trouble.

Girls Got Game: Sports Stories and Poems by Sue Macy, Henry Holt & Company, 2001

The stories and poems in this collection feature girls excelling at softball, soccer, stickball, rowing, track, and even football. The female characters challenge gender roles, explore notions of sexuality, and experience success at the sports they enjoy. Many of the stories and poems are influenced by the authors' own experiences. Some of the contributors are Virginia Euwer Wolff, Jacqueline Woodson, and Grace Butcher.

The Flip Side by Andrew Matthews, Random House, 2003

Fifteen-year-old Robert Hunt, curious about gender roles and expectations, becomes fascinated with wearing women's clothing while playing Rosalind in William Shakespeare's *As You Like It*. Not alone in his curiosity about gender, his two closest friends also question their sexuality.

Autobiography of My Dead Brother by Walter Dean Myers, art by Christopher Myers, HarperCollins, 2005

Jesse and Rise became friends when they were small boys, and it seemed as if they would be friends forever. But now that they are teenagers they seem to be growing apart. Before they go their separate ways, Jesse has agreed to write an autobiography of Rise's life, including his participation in a gang.

Keeping You a Secret by Julie Anne Peters, Little, Brown, 2003

Holland Jaeger seems to have it all: she's class president, has a cute boyfriend, and is on her way to college. When she meets Cece Goddard things change as the two girls fall in love and Holland loses the support of family and friends.

Guys Write for Guys Read edited by Jon Scieszka, Viking Penguin, 2005

This anthology includes stories, essays, comic strips, and artwork that explore growing up male in our society. A few of the many authors include Jerry Spinelli, Chris Crutcher, Walter Dean Myers, and Laurence Yep, though some of the contributors are editors and illustrators.

No Laughter Here by Rita Williams-Garcia, HarperCollins, 2003

When Victoria returns from Nigeria, her native country, Akilah wonders why she is quiet and withdrawn until she learns that Victoria was circumcised. Akilah wants to help Victoria through her pain, but she doesn't know how.

Hard Love by Ellen Wittlinger, Simon & Schuster, 1999

Sixteen-year-old John Galardi, Jr. questions his sexuality until he meets Marisol, a lesbian, and eventually falls in love with her. Hurt because he cannot pursue a relationship with Marisol, John is forced to focus on his strained relationship with his parents.

Works Cited

Blackburn, M. V., & Buckley, J. F. (2005). Teaching queer-inclusive English language arts. *English Journal*, *49*(3), 202-212.

Emert, T. (2002). An interview with Alex Sanchez, author of *Rainbow Boys*. *The Alan Review*, *29*(3), 12-14.

Schaafsma, D., Tendero, A., & Tendero, J. (1999). Making it real: Girls' stories, social change, and moral struggle. *English Journal*, *88*(5), 28-36.

Vacca, R. T., & Vacca, J. A. (2005). *Content area reading: Literacy and learning across the curriculum*. Boston: Pearson.

Chapter *6*

Religion

R ecent debates around the observance of religious holidays, predominately Christian, in our nation's schools remind us of the numerous religious practices that exist today. Many are arguing for the separation of church and state in every aspect of schooling from the prohibiting of prayer in schools to suggestions that schools should no longer observe holidays based on religious traditions. Yet, ironically, the origins of the United States' school system stems from a desire to promote religious principles. Religious groups and concerned individuals have always been vocal in their attempts to censor school materials they believe are antireligious.

Recent reports of an uproar against the teaching of evolution, the big bang theory, and other creation possibilities that are not supported by Christian principles and beliefs have made numerous teachers and librarians quite uncomfortable. Conversely, the Iraqi war and terrorist attacks by Muslims have caused some American youth to become curious about religions around the world. While we realize librarians and teachers are apprehensive about using literature with religious themes, including often anthologized excerpts from the Bible and the study of the Bible as literature, because of separation of church and state arguments, we understand that students frequenting school libraries have an interest in learning more about their own religions as well as other's religious views and practices. Despite the controversy surrounding various religions, religion remains an important part of society.

The titles in this chapter feature diverse religious beliefs and practices as well as characters who embrace, explore, challenge, and doubt the beliefs of organized religious groups and cults.

Resources on Religion

Online Resources

http://www.rsiss.net/
http://wri.leaderu.com
http://www.beliefnet.com

Other Resources

"Islam: A World Religions Resource List for Teens"
by Patty Campbell and Susan Cappetta
VOYA, 28(5), December 2005, p. 364-368

Reaching Out to Religious Youth: A Guide to Services, Programs, and Collections
by L. Kay Carman (Editor), Carol S. Reich
Libraries Unlimited, 2004

Christian Fiction: A Guide to the Genre
by John Mort
Libraries Unlimited, 2002

"Judaism: A World Religions Resource List for Teens"
by Diane P. Tuccillo
VOYA, 28(6), February 2006, p. 452-456

The Librarian's Guide to Developing Christian Fiction Collections for Young Adults
by Barbara Walker
Neal-Schuman, 2005

Integrating Multicultural Texts

Witness by Karen Hesse, Scholastic Press, 2001

Eleven characters describe the establishment of the Ku Klux Klan in this free verse novel set in Vermont in 1924.

Suggestions for Classroom Use

1. Lately, if you turn on the news, it is likely that when certain national preachers like Pat Robertson or Jerry Falwell are mentioned, the term fanatical or Christian fanatic and/or zealot is used. What does this mean? Which character(s) in the story might be labeled this way and why?

2. Which character(s) in the story might be labeled a hypocrite? Why?

3. Why does the Ku Klux Klan trouble Esther?

4. What do Esther and Leanora have in common?

5. Using resources in the library or online, find out what life was like in the United States, particularly in Vermont, during the 1920s when this story took place. What details does Hesse use to suggest that this story probably could not have taken place during another time period?

6. Do the Book-in-a-day (Allen, 2004) assignment with classmates. Form groups of 11. (You might also form groups of five and assign each member different acts.) Assign each of the 11 characters to each classmate. Classmates are only responsible for reading the sections narrated by their character. After students have read their character's section, group members must summarize the events that occurred in their sections until the entire group knows what happens in each part of the book.

Read Alike

If you like *Confessions of a Closet Catholic* (Penguin, 2005) by Sarah Darer Littman, try *With All My Heart, With All My Mind: Thirteen Stories About Growing Up Jewish* (Simon & Schuster, 1999) edited by Sandy Asher.

7. What effect, if any, do the free verse poetry and the multiple narrators have on you as a reader? How might this book have been different had it been written in prose?

8. What purpose does the Ku Klux Klan hope to serve?

9. Hesse uses non-conventional punctuation practices. Choose a passage and "edit" it. Explain why you altered it the way you did.

Armageddon Summer by Jane Yolen and Bruce Coville, Harcourt, 1998

Though not completely convinced the end of the world is near, 14-year-old Marina Marlow and 16-year-old Jed Hoskins go to Mount Weeaupcut and await Armageddon with their parents and the other Believers in Reverend Beelson's congregation.

Suggestions for Classroom Use

1. This book contains several different genres such as transcripts and e-mails. Develop a mini-multigenre paper (Romano, 2000) analyzing the book or one of the important issues in the book such as religion, cults, or friendship. Your paper should include 3-5 genres and a short preface explaining how the genres work together to make your point. Some genres you might consider are church programs/bulletins, fliers, sermons, warning signs, letters, e-mails, radio announcements, and so on. Each of your genres must help the reader understand your interpretation of the text.

2. What is a cult? Consult the dictionary and compare your definition to one you find in the dictionary.

3. How would you define the religious group in *Armageddon Summer*? Is it a cult or one of the world's religions?

4. Play Find the Fib (Manzo, Manzo, & Estes, 2001) with three of your classmates. First, each of you must write three statements based on the book: two of the statements must be true while the other one should be a

fib. Take turns reading your statements to the group as group members attempt to discern the fib.

The Baptism by Sheila P. Moses, Simon & Schuster, 2007

The Baptism, a companion novel to *The Legend of Buddy Bush* and *The Return of Buddy Bush*, introduces 12-year-old Leon, called Twin Leon, his twin brother, called Twin Luke, and his older brother, Joe Nasty. In each chapter, Leon describes his weeklong effort to go to the "mornin' bench" at revival in preparation for baptism.

Suggestions for Classroom Use

1. Before reading, complete the following Anticipation Guide (Manzo, Manzo, & Estes, 2001) by answering agree or disagree.
   a. Twelve-year-olds are capable of making decisions about religious beliefs.
   b. Everyone, even people who have been baptized, do things that are not morally right.
   c. Family members share a special bond.
   d. People are dishonest.
2. In the Author's Note, Moses explains that the children in her family were baptized when they reached 12 years old. Interview family, friends, and/or neighbors to find out if they have traditions that involve religious beliefs and practices. If so, from where did these traditions originate?
3. It has been reported that Dr. Martin Luther King, Jr. once said that the most segregated hour in the United States is eleven o' clock on Sunday morning when people are in church. How is this idea both suggested and combated in *The Baptism*?
4. Do research to find out which religions include baptisms and why.
5. Similar to the organization of the book, create a log that indicates each day of the week, from Sunday to Sunday. Under each day list the actions that prevent the twins from making their wish to be baptized known in church.

Read Alike

If you like *Sacred Places* (Penguin Young, 2000) by Philemon Sturges, try Frank Olinsky's *Buddha Book: A Meeting of Images* (Diane Publishing, 1997).

6. The term "mornin' bench" is used repeatedly. What do you think this is and how do you know?
7. What religious practices are portrayed in this book?
8. What does the word sin mean? List some examples of sins committed by Leon and his brother Joe Nasty.

Additional Titles

Rock of Ages: A Tribute to the Black Church by Tonya Bolden, illustrated by R. Gregory Christie, Random House, 2001

This book is a poetic tribute to the black church and its importance to African American history and culture.

Between Earth & Sky: Legends of Native American Sacred Places by Joseph Bruchac, illustrated by Thomas Locker, Harcourt, 1996

This book includes legends about sacred places in seven directions: east, north, south, west, above, below, and within.

Dark Sons by Nikki Grimes, Hyperion, 2005

Parallel stories tell the Biblical story of Abraham, Sarah, Isaac, Ishmael, and Hagar, while a contemporary story introduces characters in a similar plight.

Susannah by Janet Hickman, Greenwillow Books, 1998

It's 1810 just outside Lebanon, Ohio, when Susannah's growing disenchantment and suspicion of the Shaker community festers. She does not agree with many of their beliefs including the one that suggests family members distract Believers from worshiping God and Mother Ann. After she meets a distant relative, she is convinced she will never accept the Shaker's way of life.

The Secret Life of Bees by Sue Monk Kidd, Viking, 2002

Lily Owens lives with her abusive father in South Carolina until she decides to run away with her maid Rosaleen to a place she believes has answers about her mother. Once in Tiburon, they live with African American women who are beekeepers and worshipers of the Black Madonna.

I Once Was a Monkey: Stories Buddha Told by Jeanne M. Lee, Farrar, Straus and Giroux, 1999

Seeking refuge during a monsoon, a monkey huddles in a cave alongside several other animals while listening to six stories, Jatakas or birth stories, once told by Buddha. The stories, which feature one of the types of animals in the cave, include lessons about friendship, endurance, patience, and logical thinking.

Read Alike

If you like *Once I Was a Monkey: Stories Buddha Told* (Farrar, Straus and Giroux, 1999) by Jeanne M. Lee, try Caldecott winner, John Muth's, *Zen Shorts* (Scholastic, 2005).

Confessions of a Closet Catholic by Sarah Darer Littman, Penguin, 2005

Justine Silver, annoyed because her family does not take her seriously when she wants to keep kosher, becomes interested in learning more about other religions such as Roman Catholicism. When her Bubbe dies, she takes her advice and learns more about Judaism.

Habibi by Naomi Shihab Nye, Simon & Schuster, 1997

Liyanna Abboud is devastated because her family is moving from St. Louis, Missouri to Jerusalem near where her father once lived. While there, she learns about her Arab heritage and questions the anger between Jews and Palestinians.

God Went to Beauty School by Cynthia Rylant, HarperCollins, 2003

In this novel in verse, the author imagines what God might do if He came to earth. Would He be a nail tech in His own salon, own a dog, ride in a boat, rollerblade, or watch cable television?

I Believe in Water: Twelve Brushes with Religion edited by Marilyn Singer, HarperCollins, 2000

Twelve stories by popular young adult writers (e.g., Jacqueline Woodson, Naomi Shihab Nye, Joyce Carol Thomas, Kyoko Mori) explore a number of religions and spiritual beliefs including Jehovah's Witness, Buddhism, and Judaism.

Dust by Arthur G. Slade, Random House, 2003

Eleven-year-old Robert Steelgate is the only one in his small community in Saskatchewan who realizes that a stranger, Abram Harsich, who claims to have the power to make a badly needed rainmaking machine, is actually kidnapping children and enchanting the town's citizens. The book is set in the 1930s in the middle of a drought, and Biblical references are included.

The Journey by Sarah Stewart, illustrated by David Small, Farrar, Straus and Giroux, 2001

Diary entries document Hannah's first trip to Chicago. Hannah returns to her life in her Amish community after visiting places in the city she had never heard of before.

Sacred Places by Philemon Sturges, illustrated by Giles Laroche, Penguin Young, 2000

Hindu, Buddhist, Islamic, Jewish and Christian sacred places all over the world are illustrated in this picture book. The illustrations convey the significance of each place of worship.

Blankets by Craig Thompson, Top Shelf, 2003

Semi-autobiographical, this graphic novel depicts Craig's Christian upbringing in Wisconsin. While young he is devoted to worshipping God and studying the Bible, but adulthood brings questions about the validity of his religion. Adult situations and some nudity might make this book more appropriate for mature readers.

Hush by Jacqueline Woodson, Penguin, 2002

After Toswiah Green's father testifies against corrupt fellow police officers, her family's lives change. They are entered into the witness protection program where they are given new names, new lives. Toswiah's mother becomes a Jehovah's Witness in order to cope with her new circumstances.

Works Cited

Allen, J. (2004). *Tools for teaching content literacy*. Portland, Maine: Stenhouse.

Manzo, A. V., Manzo, U. C., & Estes, T. H. (2001). *Content area literacy: Interactive teaching for active learning*. NY: Wiley.

Romano, T. (2000). *Blending genre, altering style: Writing multigenre papers*. Portsmouth, NH: Boynton/Cook.

 Collaboration Ideas

Religious and Cultural

Many public schools shy away from any mention of religion, but for some students, religion is a major part of their home lives. Denying any mention of that part of their lives closes off part of the whole child approach to education.

Ideas for Collaboration

Assign mythology stories for reading. Ask students to choose a major world religion, and find an event that can be translated into a story, including dialogue. Encourage students to choose a religion different from their own. CORRELATION: Geography, Language Arts (Writing), Ancient History (Mythology).

Using an outline map of the world, color in various religions documented by authoritative research sources to be the major religion in that country. Assign and research these religions, including fiction resources if available. Instead of assigning each research group a religion to investigate and present, assign each to choose a theme and investigate it across religions, such as creation, afterlife, worship rituals, holy days.

Chapter 7

Socio-Economics

S ocial class adds yet another dimension to the diversity that exists in the world. It is largely determined by an individual's educational background, profession, and yearly earnings (Persell, 1989). Most people agree that economic inequality exists in our society. There are a number of class groupings from wealthy and upper middle class to middle class, working class, and the poor. Many of today's families across the United States live below the poverty line. According to Beach and Marshall (1990), half of all black children and four out of ten Latina/o children live in poverty.

Since the founding of our country, it has been thought that an individual has complete control over his or her potential to obtain wealth, but now we know that there are factors, such as industrial downsizing, cost of living increases, repression, and even natural disasters, that can contribute to poverty despite efforts of self-reliance.

In 2005 when Hurricane Katrina landed in the gulf coast, the media portrayed an America divided by race and class. Some critics suggest that rescue efforts in New Orleans were minimized for those considered of less value, the poor. As a result of Hurricanes Katrina and Rita, over 1,000 people died and thousands suddenly became destitute and homeless. Socio-economic disparity is a reality that cannot be ignored.

The books in this chapter offer a glimpse into the varied social classes that exist in society. The authors address issues around socio-economics in ways that encourage readers to understand class issues, and possibly, move toward contributing to social change. Some of the topics covered include homelessness, unemployment, underemployment, welfare, migrant farming, and upward mobility.

Online Bibliographies

http://scholar.lib.vt.edu/ejournals/ALAN/spring96/mcdonald.html
http://falcon.jmu.edu/~ramseyil/asian.htm
http://falcon.jmu.edu/~ramseyil/mulgay.htm
http://www.nea.org/readacross/resources/aabooks.html
http://www.wingluke.org/bibliography.html
http://www.cynthialeitichsmith.com/lit_resources/diversity/asian_am/
asian_am.html
http://www.isomedia.com/homes/jmele/joe.html
http://falcon.jmu.edu/~ramseyil/mulapach.htm

Integrating Multicultural Texts

Elegy on the Death of Cesar Chavez: A Poem by Rudolfo Anaya, illustrated by Gaspar Enriquez, Cinco Puntos, 2000

Anaya's poem written in honor of Cesar Chavez concludes with an informative biography and timeline of important events. The poem reminds readers of the important work Chavez accomplished as well as the work that still needs to be done. The mixed media illustrations are a thought-provoking extension of the text.

Suggestions for Classroom Use

1. What is an elegy? Visit <http://www.uncp.edu/home/canada/work/allam/general/glossary.htm> for a detailed definition of elegy or consult a dictionary of literary terms. When you learn what an elegy is and the form it takes, choose a person in history who is important to you or interests you and write an elegy in that person's honor.

2. The author includes an excerpt from Percy Bysshe Shelley's "Adonais: An Elegy on the Death of John Keats." Read the poem at <http://rpo.library.utoronto.ca/poem/1879.html>. Find out more about John Keats and the influence he had on Shelley. Based on this book, what influence did Cesar Chavez have on the author?

3. Dolores Huerta helped Cesar Chavez establish the National Farm Workers Association. Consult a reference source to learn more about Huerta.

4. Search major newspapers such as *The New York Times* for articles about the ceremony President Bill Clinton had bestowing the Medal of Freedom to Cesar Chavez in August of 1994. Write an acceptance speech influenced by what you know about Cesar Chavez's character, life, and work. Read the biography that concludes *Elegy on the Death of Cesar Chavez* and search <www.ufw.org> for a bibliography of books about him.

5. Visit <www.ufw.org> to learn more about Cesar Chavez and the history of the United Farm Workers.

6. Use a reference source to find out more about the illustrator, Gaspar Enriquez. Has he illustrated other books since the publication in 2000 of *Elegy on the Death of Cesar Chavez*? If so, what are they about and how do the illustrations compare? Are different media used?

 Read Alike

If you like *Chill Wind* (Farrar, Straus and Giroux, 2002) by Janet McDonald, try her novel titled *Twists and Turns* (Farrar, Straus and Giroux, 2003).

7. Identify three metaphors in Anaya's poem. How do the metaphors add to the meaning of the poem?

Seedfolks by Paul Fleischman, HarperCollins, 1997

Set in Cleveland, Ohio in an impoverished neighborhood, several strangers from different cultural backgrounds and ages come together to convert a dilapidated plot of land into a beautiful garden. Though the neighbors are initially suspicious of each other, their stories eventually intertwine as they ban together to maintain the garden that a young Vietnamese unwittingly begins by planting beans in honor of her deceased father. Thirteen voices make up the thin novel that raises issues about poverty, neglect, honor, pride, heritage, and love.

Suggestions for Classroom Use

1. Consider the theme, setting, and characterization found in *Seedfolks*. Find a poem that might accompany this book and explain the similarities that exist between the two genres.

2. How would you categorize *Seedfolks*? What genre is it? Explain.

3. How is *Seedfolks* a book about community building across cultural difference and socio-economics?

4. List examples of social action suggested in *Seedfolks*.

5. Describe three of the characters' motivations for planting a garden.

6. Take a virtual tour of some of Cleveland's neighborhoods at <http://www.city.cleveland.oh.us/around_town/map/neighborhood/neighborhood.html>. How would you describe the history of the neighborhood in *Seedfolks*? What would you name the neighborhood?

The Circuit: Stories from the Life of a Migrant Child by Francisco Jiménez, University of New Mexico Press, 1997

Based on the author's youth, this collection of stories begins in Mexico and describes Francisco's family's illegal immigration into the United States where they find jobs as migrant laborers. The family faces poverty and the constant fear of being deported.

Suggestions for Classroom Use

1. There are numerous Spanish terms and phrases throughout the book. Use the terms to create a Spanish/English dictionary.

2. Using a research source, find out about child labor laws in the United States. Are there laws specifically for agricultural work?

3. Read *Breaking Through*, also by Francisco Jiménez, to learn more about Panchito and his family.

4. Read the picture book version of chapter 3, "Inside Out," titled *La Mariposa* (Houghton Mifflin, 1998) by Francisco Jiménez. Does the illustrator's interpretation of the story come close to the images you saw in your mind as you read? Choose one of the other chapters of the book to illustrate with drawings or pictures from magazines.

5. Do research to find out the annual wages of a migrant worker.

In the Reseach | **The Migrant Experience**

York analyzes over 25 books in several genres, including poetry and nonfiction that depict Mexican American migrants. She suggests several activities, projects, and discussion topics teachers and librarians can use when teaching literature that features migrant experiences. Some of the titles discussed are *Elegy on the Death of Cesar Chavez* (Cinco Puntos, 2000) by Rudolfo Anaya, *La Mariposa* (Houghton Mifflin, 1998) and *The Circuit: Stories from the Life of a Migrant Child* (University of New Mexico Press, 1997) by Francisco Jiménez, and *Esperanza Rising* (Scholastic, 2001) by Pam Munoz Ryan.

York, Sherry. (2002). The migrant experience in the works of Mexican American writers. *The Alan Review, 29*(3), 22-25.

Pictures of Hollis Woods by Patricia Reilly Giff, Random House, 2002

Hollis Woods, a gifted artist and habitual runaway, is in and out of foster homes until she finds a family that wants to make her one of their own. Her happiness dissipates, however, when an accident occurs for which Hollis feels responsible.

Suggestions for Classroom Use

1. Create a series of drawings based on the descriptions of Hollis's drawings. Write an interpretation of the drawings.

2. Investigate the minimum amount of money a typical family needs to earn in your town. Create a budget that includes typical mortgage, insurance, and car payments as well as food and clothing expenses.

3. Investigate the availability of jobs in your town. What education is required, and what skills are needed?

4. In the past, children without parents were placed in orphanages. Investigate the history of state homes for children in your state. What was life like living there? Do orphanages (or an equivalent such as a children's home) still exist in your state?

5. Find a list of famous people who were foster children or who grew up in orphanages. Read their biographies (i.e., *Finding Fish* by screenwriter and poet, Antwone Fisher) and compare their experiences to Hollis's experiences.

6. Investigate the college you would like to attend some day and retrieve the application. If Hollis Woods were planning to attend that college, what would she write in her college entrance essay?

7. If you are interested in books about foster care, try *Teenage Voices from the Foster Care System* edited by Al Desetta.

Select Awards & Honors
Newbery Honor 2003
ALA Best Books for Young Adults 2003
ALA Notable Children's Books 2003

In the Reseach	Adrian Fogelin's Fiction in the Middle School

Bowman and Edenfield read Fogelin's *Crossing Jordan* (Peachtree, 2000) with students who live in Tallahassee, Florida, the novel's setting. In Bowman and Edenfield's hands the study of the novel became a community-wide event. Preservice teachers in Bowman's class created interdisciplinary lesson plans (including physical education, art, and science) around the novel and worked with middle school classroom teachers to implement them. Some of the plans included group work and the use of technology while others encouraged using the track to study distance, rate, and time in math class. Lesson plans in music focus on gospel hymns and Southern music themes.

Bowman, C., & Edenfield, R. (2003). Adrian Fogelin's fiction in the middle school classroom. *The Alan Review, 30*(2), 13-15.

Kira-Kira by Cynthia Kadohata, Simon & Schuster, 2004

When Katie Takeshima and her family move from Iowa to Georgia where there are few Japanese families, they are faced with prejudice. Her sister Lynn teaches her to look forward to those things that are kira-kira, glittering and shiny, instead of focusing on adversity, including poverty.

Suggestions for Classroom Use

1. Katie reads excerpts from Lynn's diary, but what if Katie had kept a diary of her own? Choose an important scene from the novel and write a journal entry from Katie's perspective.

2. Explain how sibling relationships are important in this novel. Consider Katie's relationship with her siblings as well as her father's relationship with his brother.

3. Lynn has lymphoma. What are the symptoms? What treatments/medications are available?

4. Using evidence from the novel, explain why buying a house is so important to Katie's family. What do they sacrifice in order to obtain this part of the American dream?

5. Keep a chart of the race, class, and gender discrimination the characters face. Write a short paper explaining how Katie's family coped with multiple types of prejudice. Include evidence from the text.

6. How does Mrs. Takeshima's attitude toward union organizers change? Why does her attitude change?

Select Awards & Honors

John Newbery Medal
Asian/Pacific American Award for Literature

Additional Titles

The House on Mango Street by Sandra Cisneros, Arte Publico, 1984

Short vignettes focus on the life of Esperanza, a poor, Latina adolescent, growing up in a Chicago neighborhood. Esperanza looks at her surroundings through the eyes of someone determined to venture to other places in pursuit of her dreams before returning home to help others.

Growing Up Poor: A Literary Anthology edited by Robert Coles and Randy Testa with Michael Coles, New Press, 2001

This anthology features 20th century American poems and novel excerpts about poverty by writers as diverse as Langston Hughes, Luis J. Rodriquez, Sherman Alexie, and Zora Neale Hurston. Most of the familiar selections are among the celebrated works of these authors.

Burning Up by Caroline B. Cooney, Delacorte, 1999

While working on a class project, Macey Clare uncovers some disturbing information about racism and hatred within her comfortable, white middle class community. The most shocking truth she learns is that white privilege often prevents some from helping those who are discriminated against.

Bucking the Sarge by Christopher Paul Curtis, Random House, 2004

Luther T. Farrell's mother (The Sarge) has always made it her business to find ways to make money. Now, after taking care of men in his mother's adult rehabilitation home without pay, Luther has found a way to make sure his mother funds his college education. He uses his middle school science fair project to expose her underhanded dealings to all of Flint, Michigan.

Crossing Jordan by Adrian Fogelin, Peachtree, 2000

Cass's working class family isn't happy when an African American family moves in next door, but her curiosity and genuine interest in Jemmie helps the two families forge a friendship. The girls also bond because of their interest in *Jane Eyre* and flair for running.

Soul Moon Soup by Lindsay Lee Johnson, Boyd Mills, 1998

Phoebe Rose's father has disappeared, leaving her and her mother homeless. As the novel in verse progresses, she finds it difficult to hold on to the things she loves like art and her mother. Destitute and full of despair, Phoebe moves in with her grandmother until her mother is able to support her financially.

Spite Fences by Trudy Krisher, Delacorte, 1994

Thirteen-year-old Maggie Pugh is a part of a poor family in rural Georgia, a place deeply divided by race and class. Maggie feels it is up to her to use her strength and determination to make a difference.

Parrot in the Oven: Mi Vida by Victor Martinez, HarperCollins, 1996

Manny Hernandez wants to be a man, but he has so few role models living in poverty in the projects, the task seems impossible without the help of being affiliated with a gang. Manny doesn't want the dangers of gang-related activities to ruin his hopes for a better life.

Chill Wind by Janet McDonald, Farrar, Straus and Giroux, 2002

Nineteen-year-old Aisha Ingram is a single mother who must work in New York City's workfare program after her welfare benefits end. Desperate, Aisha attempts to pursue a modeling career.

The Glass Café or, The Stripper and the State: How My Mother Started a War with the System That Made Us Kind of Rich and a Little Bit Famous by Gary Paulsen, Random House, 2003

When Tony's mom, Al, takes him to work with her at the Kitty Kat Club where she is an exotic dancer, he decides to draw some of the women. His art teacher, excited about Tony's interpretation of the human body, enters his sketches in a competition, causing alarm for a concerned citizen who alerts social services. A caseworker investigates and eventually takes Tony out of his mother's custody, but Al, who is a college graduate, fights to get her son back and somehow wins a lucrative settlement.

The Way a Door Closes by Hope Anita Smith, illustrations by Shane W. Evans, Henry Holt, 2003

In 34 poems, protagonist, Cameron James, describes the changes in his family's finances and well being after his father abandons them. Though Cameron wants to be the man of the house, his mother wants him to enjoy his childhood.

Sparrow by Sherri L. Smith, Random House, 2006

Seventeen-year-old Kendall Washington is all alone and destitute in Chicago since her grandmother died and her only living relative, Aunt Janet, doesn't want to help her. After traveling to New Orleans, she meets Miss Clare and her daughter, Evie, who has muscular dystrophy. The three form a family, helping each other during difficult times.

Buried Onions by Gary Soto, Harcourt, 1997

Attending City College doesn't seem practical to Eddie since he is consumed with surviving in Fresno, California where friends and relatives are dying rapidly and jobs, food, and shelter are difficult to obtain. Now his aunt wants him to avenge her son's death. Eddie must decide how and if he is going to make a life for himself that doesn't involve poverty and violence.

Learning the Game by Kevin Waltman, Scholastic, 2005

Though Nate Gilman is a popular athlete who comes from a rich family, he decides to join in when his friends break into the Sigma Chi fraternity house. Though he's unsure of why he participated in the crime, he knows he has to eventually accept responsibility for his actions.

I Hadn't Meant to Tell You This by Jacqueline Woodson, Delacorte, 1994

Though 13-year-old Marie lives amongst the black middle class, she is drawn to Lena, a poor, white girl who is being abused by her father. In *Lena*, the sequel to *I Hadn't Meant to Tell You This*, Lena and her sister are homeless as they attempt to find a safe harbor away from their abusive father.

Works Cited

Beach, R. W., & Marshall, J. D. (1990). *Teaching literature in the secondary school*. California: Wadsworth.

Bowman, C., & Edenfield, R. (2003). Adrian Fogelin's fiction in the middle school classroom. *The Alan Review, 30*(2), 13-15.

Persell, C. H. (1989). Social class and educational equality. In J. A. Banks & C. A. M. Banks (Eds.), *Multicultural education: Issues and perspectives* (pp. 68-82). Boston: Allyn and Bacon.

York, Sherry. (2002). The migrant experience in the works of Mexican American writers. *The Alan Review, 29*(3), 22-25.

Chapter *8*

Geographic Orientation

M igration has been an important aspect within various cultural groups. For example, the migration of large numbers of African Americans to the North from the rural South during the early twentieth century meant job opportunities and, in some cases, a modest amount of freedom from racism. The same is true today as Hispanic and Asian Americans, once thought to only occupy large states such as California and New York, are now making their homes in the Midwest and on the southern east coast in states like North Carolina and Virginia where opportunities for employment exist. Some people believe our identities are shaped, in part, by where we grew up.

The idea of taking a journey, whether real or metaphoric, coupled with a sense of place, or geographical locale, plays a role in most of the books in this chapter. The texts seem to ask many questions: What is it like growing up in the south, the Midwest, on the west coast, or in an urban or rural setting? What kinds of experiences do people have? Which experiences transcend geographical divides? What kinds of opportunities are available to individuals simply based upon geographic location? These are prominent themes in the literature included in this chapter.

Integrating Multicultural Texts

Spinning Through the Universe by Helen Frost, Frances Foster, 2004

This novel in verse includes different voices from room 214, Mrs. Williams's fifth grade class. Some students face poverty, abuse, homelessness, and death while growing up in the inner city while others are gifted in math, fall in love, or create art. A useful author's note explaining the poetic forms used throughout the book is included.

Suggestions for Classroom Use

1. Most of Naomi's poems are haikus. Use one as a model to create your own haiku about life, particularly things related to the seasons and/or nature, in the city.

2. Write a poem by taking on the persona of one of your classmates. Share it with your peers to see if they can guess who the poem is about.

3. Research one of the social issues (i.e., homelessness, poverty, abuse) in the book. How does your research enhance your understanding of the issue?

 Read Alike

If you like *Making Up Megaboy* (DK Publishing, 1998) by Virginia Walter, try *Shooter* (HarperCollins, 2004) by Walter Dean Myers or *The Brimstone Journals* (Candlewick Press, 2001) by Ron Koertge.

4. Create a skit including several of the characters and then perform it in front of the class.

5. Using evidence from the text, explain how Mrs. Williams feels about her students and how they feel about her.

6. Search the Children in Urban America Web site at <http://xserver1.its.mu.edu/index.html> to learn more about how youth live in urban areas in the United States.

My Chinatown by Kam Max, HarperCollins, 2001

This book documents a year in the life of a boy living in Chinatown in New York City. The book is based on the author/illustrator's own memories of growing up in the city.

Suggestions for Classroom Use

1. Using examples from the poem, describe the protagonist's feelings about Chinatown.

2. Describe what you learned about Chinatown from reading this book.

3. List the things the protagonist misses about Hong Kong.

4. Write a poem or descriptive paragraph about one of your favorite places.

5. When authors use personification, they describe inanimate objects as if they are human. Find several examples of personification throughout the book.

Come with Me: Poems for a Journey by Naomi Shihab Nye, illustrated by Dan Yaccarino, Greenwillow, 2000

What do we mean when we say we are going on a journey? Is it real or imaginary? The 16 poems in this picture book explore the multifaceted nature of the word journey.

Suggestions for Classroom Use

1. What types of poems are in this picture book? Make a chart of poetic terms including metaphor, personification, alliteration, and simile. Under each heading, jot down examples of each poetic element from the poems in this book. Use the examples to help you create metaphors, similes, alliteration, and personification in your own writing.

2. Have you ever been on an imaginary journey? Where did you go? When did you go? Why did you go?

3. Make a list of all of the places you'd like to visit someday and explain why you want to visit these places. Then go on the Internet to see if there are virtual trips available.

4. Read one of Nye's books written for teenagers or adults. How are the themes similar and/or different? Do you find that the journey theme recurs throughout her work? Why might this theme be an important one to explore?

5. Authors often write forewords or afterwords for books in order to explain their intentions, or their purpose for writing the book. Find three books with either forewords or afterwords. What do the authors include? Then write a foreword or an afterword for *Come with Me*.

> **Read Alike**
>
> If you like Helen Frost's *Spinning Through the Universe* (Frances Foster, 2004), try her book, *Keesha's House* (Farrar, Straus and Giroux, 2003).

Making Up Megaboy by Virginia Walter, illustrated by Katrina Roeckelein, DK Publishing, 1998

Everyone is shocked when 13-year-old Robbie Jones kills Mr. Jae Lin Koh, the owner of the neighborhood liquor store in California. Told from multiple perspectives, each character looks deeply into Robbie's character for a motive.

Suggestions for Classroom Use

1. Read *Monster* and *Shooter* by Walter Dean Myers and *The Brimstone Journals* by Ron Koertge. Compare and contrast the main characters in these books with Robbie. Why do they turn to violence?

Read Alike

If you like *Rain Is Not My Indian Name* (HarperCollins, 2001) by Cynthia Leitich Smith, try her book *Indian Shoes* (HarperCollins, 2002).

2. Explain Robbie's fascination with his comic book hero. How is Robbie Megaboy?

3. Why did Robbie kill Mr. Koh? Write a letter from Robbie describing his motive. Don't forget to address the letter to someone (i.e., his mother, Mrs. Koh, the media, Tara, and so forth.)

4. Critique the illustrations. Are the illustrations necessary? If so, explain how the illustrations contribute to the meaning of the text. Do the illustrations provide information that the text doesn't? What do you notice about fonts/typeface? What do you think the change in fonts/typeface mean?

5. Describe the setting in *Making Up Megaboy*? Do you think something similar could happen in a rural setting?

6. The book reads like media. Create a script for a news program that explores some of the issues addressed in the book.

Additional Titles

The Heart of a Chief by Joseph Bruchac, Dial, 1998

Chris Nicola is a Penacook Indian growing up on a reservation. He tries to convince the students and administrators at his school and the people on his reservation to preserve Native American history and culture.

The Tequila Worm by Viola Canales, Random House, 2005

Sofia's life in the barrio of McAllen, Texas changes when she earns a scholarship to Saint Luke's Episcopal School, a prestigious boarding school hundreds of miles away from her family. Though she does not want to leave the comfort of her barrio, she knows she must take advantage of an educational opportunity too few adolescents get.

Walk Two Moons by Sharon Creech, HarperCollins, 1994

Thirteen-year-old Salamanca Tree Hiddle, or Sal, travels from Ohio to Idaho with her grandparents looking for her mother, who had abandoned her family. The book contains several layers of story that reveal the humor, love, and sorrow that surrounds Salamanca.

Bang! by Sharon Flake, Hyperion, 2005

Influenced by African tribal practices, 13-year-old Mann's father decides to teach him to be a man by leaving him stranded in the woods with his best friend, Kee-lee. When Mann and Kee-lee return to their urban environment filled with random shooting, Mann's father abandons him again. He has to learn to survive in the brutal setting that killed his younger brother without the help of his parents.

Cinnamon Girl: Letters Found Inside a Cereal Box by Juan Felipe Herrera, Joanna Cotler, 2005

Written in poetry and letters, the story uncovers the relationship between 10th-grader Yolanda and her Uncle DJ, who is rescued after the destruction of the World Trade Center. Yolanda laments about living in Iowa where she was one of a few Puerto Ricans before living in New York.

Aleutian Sparrow by Karen Hesse, Margaret K. McElderry, 2003

Vera's father is white and her mother is Aleut. During World War II, Vera, her mother, and the other Aleutian people in their community were forced to relocate to camps in the forests of Alaska. Her father, however, was allowed to remain home because he was white. He managed to protect their property from thieves, but many of the others living in the camps lost their valuables.

Fishing for Chickens: Short Stories About Rural Youth edited by Jim Heynen, Persea, 2001

This collection includes 16 short stories set in rural locations throughout the United States, including Mississippi, North Carolina, and Hawaii. Prominent writers like Alice Walker, Wallace Stegner and Tomas Rivera's stories are alongside those by lesser known authors such as Rebecca Rule, Nancy K. Brown, and Kathleen Tyau.

Necessary Roughness by Marie G. Lee, HarperCollins, 1996

Sixteen-year-old Chan Kim doesn't want to move from Los Angeles to Minnesota with his family, but he doesn't have a choice. Being the only Asian family amongst a state filled with whites proves difficult for the Kim's, especially Chan. Football seems to be the only way he can prove to everyone that he can fit in.

The Beast by Walter Dean Myers, Scholastic, 2003

Anthony Witherspoon, or Spoon, spends his last year of high school at Wallingford Academy, a prestigious boarding school in New England. When he returns to Harlem during a school break, he sees his old neighborhood from a different perspective. His girlfriend is on drugs and some of his friends are experimenting with gangs and taking unhealthy risks.

Music from a Place Called Half Moon by Jerrie Oughton, Houghton Mifflin, 1995

Set during the summer of 1956 in Half Moon, North Carolina, 13-year-old Edie Jo Houp, and the rest of the community, is upset when her father invites Native American and biracial children to the church's Vacation Bible School. Her attitude changes, however, when she befriends a Native American classmate.

Rain Is Not My Indian Name by Cynthia Leitich Smith, HarperCollins, 2001

Set in a small Kansas town, 14-year-old Cassidy Rain Berghoff is interested in both her white and Native American heritage, but she feels uncomfortable when her Aunt Georgia asks her to attend a camp for Native American youth. Hoping to overcome the loss of her mother and close friend, she agrees to photograph events during the camp for the local newspaper.

Big City Cool: Short Stories About Urban Youth edited by M. Jerry Weiss and Helen S. Weiss, Persea, 2002

Fourteen stories by well-known authors such as Walter Dean Myers, Judith Ortiz Cofer, Eleanora Tate, and Amy Tan are set in locales as diverse as Boston, Las Vegas, Cleveland, and Morehead City, North Carolina. A particularly interesting story, "Alone and All Together," by Joseph Geha focuses on the pain of September 11, 2001 for Americans in general and Arab Americans in particular.

Like Sisters on the Homefront by Rita Williams-Garcia, Lodestar, 1995

Fourteen-year-old Gayle Whitaker's mother sends her to live with relatives in the south after she aborts her second pregnancy. While in Georgia, she learns family history and forms a relationship with her family.

Locomotion by Jacqueline Woodson, Putnam, 2003

Lonnie Collins Motion, or Locomotion, has known mostly heartache in his twelve years of living in an urban setting. His parents' death and separation from his sister have him wondering about family, love, and belonging. He reaches a turning point when his teacher shows him how writing poetry can help ease his pain.

Sky Scrape/City Scape: Poems of City Life selected by Jane Yolen, illustrated by Ken Condon, Boyds Mills, 1996

This collection of poems in a picture book format, celebrate life in the city. The poems are by well-known writers such as Langston Hughes, Lee Bennett Hopkins, Myra Cohn Livingstone, and Eve Merriam.

Chapter 9

Language/ Country of Origin

According to the United States Census Bureau reports in 2003, 33.5 million people in the United States were foreign-born. Most were natives of Latin America or Asia. In 2004, over 900,000 immigrants entered the United States, many of which speak multiple languages. Debates about the use of languages other than English in the classroom seem to ring louder today than ever. Ebonics debates and talk amongst teacher educators about the ease of codeswitching and valuing students' home languages as bridges to learning standard English also abound. Yet, the public high schools alone in Bridgeport, Connecticut, for example, contain over 5,000 students who speak over 60 languages (Winik, 2006). Today, Hispanics are one of the largest cultural groups in the United States. Efforts to make Spanish available on the labels of goods, over the telephone, and in the media indicate the United States is gradually embracing multilingualism.

However, when some students speak other languages, they are told that United States classrooms are "English only" spaces. Inviting young people to celebrate language diversity can only begin when they are allowed the freedom to speak home languages free of guilt and ridicule as many of the characters in the following books do. The main characters in the following books, some of which are considered immigrant tales, celebrate language diversity by acknowledging the importance of speaking multiple languages and the cultural alliance that exists between a speaker and those who speak his/her native language. Some of the books focus on the inner turmoil associated with learning English as a second language as the characters feel their language is viewed as inferior. Most of the books include a glossary complete with pronunciation guides while others make the meaning of non-English words clear and concise in the body of the text.

Integrating Multicultural Texts

Cesar: ¡Sí, Se Puede! (Yes, We Can!) by Carmen T. Bernier-Grand, illustrated by David Diaz, Marshall Cavendish, 2004

This book provides an overview of major events in Cesario Estrada Chavez's (Cesar Chavez) life. Chavez left school after 8th grade to help support his family. After serving in the United States Navy, he was forced to return to working in farms because no one would hire him. He eventually began giving speeches for the Community Service Organization and encouraging Mexican Americans to vote. Fully aware of the poor working conditions and wages of farm workers, during the 1950s he helped organize the first union for farm workers, The National Farm Worker Association renamed the United Farm Workers. The book includes an overview of Chavez's life and work, a glossary, bibliography, and source-notes.

Suggestions for Classroom Use

Read Alike

If you like *Letters from Rifka* (Henry Holt, 1992) by Karen Hesse, try *Maggie's Door* (Random House, 2003) by Patricia Reilly Giff.

1. Chavez's teacher tells him not to speak Spanish in class because he is in America, but Chavez believes that knowledge and facility of more than one language indicates wisdom. Do you agree with Chavez or his teacher? Explain.

2. Offer examples of how Chavez challenged injustices.

3. How would you describe Chavez's political and activist philosophies? Who influenced his way of thinking?

4. Look closely at the poems. Can you identify any poetic elements (i.e., simile, metaphor, alliteration)?

5. The illustrations were created using Adobe Photoshop. Examine the illustrations in the book. Do they seem to extend the text? What kinds of images do you believe would best accommodate the poems?

Copper Sun by Sharon Draper, Simon & Schuster, 2006

Fifteen-year-old Amiri is taken from her village in Africa, shackled, and shipped to the Carolina colony. Sold to the Derby's, Amiri must settle down to a life of slavery, which unfortunately includes murder, torture, and rape. In alternate chapters Amiri and a white indentured servant named Polly, who is responsible for teaching Amiri English, describe the events that lead up to their close friendship and eventual escape from slavery to Fort Mose, Florida, a Spanish colony. A list of sources and an afterword written for teachers ends the book.

Suggestions for Classroom Use

1. Read Countee Cullen's poem, "Heritage." How are the themes in the novel and the poem similar?

2. Resistance is a common theme in novels about oppression. How do the characters resist oppression?

3. Use a reference source to learn about the middle passage.

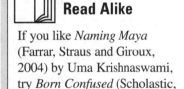

Read Alike

If you like *Naming Maya* (Farrar, Straus and Giroux, 2004) by Uma Krishnaswami, try *Born Confused* (Scholastic, 2002) by Tanuja Desai Hidier.

4. Compare Draper's depiction of the middle passage to Toni Morrison's in *Beloved* and to Robert Hayden's poem, "Middle Passage."

5. Amiri and Polly both offer their perspectives of similar events and issues on the plantation. Write a brief paper explaining Amiri and Polly's similarities and differences.

Letters from Rifka by Karen Hesse, Henry Holt, 1992

It is 1919 when 12-year-old Rifka Nebrot and her family attempt to escape her home in Berdichev where they live in poverty and danger. Her parents have managed to keep their five sons out of the Russian army thus angering the Russians. Now the oldest sons who live in America are awaiting their arrival. After being afflicted with typhus, everyone emigrates except Rifka who is not allowed into the United States because she has ringworm. The novel is based on one of the author's relatives' immigration experiences.

Suggestions for Classroom Use

1. Keep a log of Rifka's travels from the Ukraine to Ellis Island. Use a reference source to find a map or create one of your own.

2. Each letter in the book begins with an excerpt from a poem by Alexander Pushkin. Choose four of the excerpts and write about how the lines of poetry connect with the content of Rifka's letter.

3. Just when it seems that Rifka has a solution to her problem, the author creates another conflict she must resolve. Draw a t-chart. On one side, keep a record of the problems that arise for Rifka, and on the other side, record the resolution. Now try writing a story of your own. After you have settled on a few characters, an object or accomplishment the main character wants to obtain, and a setting, brainstorm a list of possible obstacles that might interfere with the main character's attempt to achieve his or her goals.

4. Visit the United States Citizenship and Immigration Services Web site at <www.USCIS.gov>. How does one become a lawful permanent resident in the United States? What paths of immigration are available to persons seeking a green card (i.e., immigration through employment or international adoption)?

5. Is Rifka a hero? Why or Why not?

6. Pretend you are Tovah and you have just received one of Rifka's letters. Reply to Rifka. Ask her questions about her journey, and tell her how your life has changed since she left for America.

7. In the United States, racial passing, which occurs when a member of a racial group pretends to be a member of another group (for example, very light skinned blacks who pass for white), has been debated and scrutinized. Here, Rifka attempts to pass. Why does she attempt to pass, and is she successful? How does language use make passing accessible to Rifka?

Read Alike

If you like An Na's *A Step from Heaven* (Boyds Mills Press, 2001), try *First Crossing: Stories About Teen Immigrants* (Candlewick Press, 2004) edited by Donald R. Gallo.

Select Awards & Honors
National Jewish Book Award
Sydney Taylor Book Award
Christopher Book Award

Yellow Star by Jennifer Roy, Marshall Cavendish, 2006

Written in free-verse, this novel is based on the experiences of Holocaust survivor, Sylvia (formerly Syvia) Perlmutter. After living in Lodz ghetto in Poland for over five years with her parents and sister, Dora, Perlmutter became one of only a few children who made it out of Lodz alive. The book includes an author's note, timeline, and brief historical details that preface each of the five sections of the book.

Though she spent most of her teen years in Paris, France, she eventually immigrated to the United States and settled in Albany, New York. She is a volunteer at the United States Holocaust Memorial Museum in Washington, DC where she teaches others about Holocaust history.

Suggestions for Classroom Use

1. Voice is an important aspect of writing. The author of this novel begins by capturing the voice of four-year-old Syvia. As Syvia matures, her voice also matures. Highlight or write down words, lines, and/or passages that capture Syvia at different ages in the novel. Look at a story you have written. How might you vary the voice of characters in your own writing?

2. Browse the United States Holocaust Museum's online encyclopedia at <http://www.ushmm.org/wlc/en/>. What difficulties did refugees seeking sanctuary in the United States face during the Holocaust?

3. Visit <http://www.ushmm.org/wlc/en/> to learn about Lodz ghetto. Observe the maps. When was Lodz established? How many people were housed there? Describe the living conditions in Lodz. How did the conditions there compare to those in Warsaw?

4. How did the Perlmutters attempt to resist oppression?

5. Explore <http://www.ushmm.org/museum/exhibit/focus/uprising/>. How did people detained at the Warsaw ghetto initiate an uprising? What other acts of resistance occurred?

Additional Titles

Finding Miracles by Julia Alvarez, Alfred A. Knopf, 2004

Vermont resident Milly Kaufman feels uncomfortable around her classmate, Pablo Bolívar, a recent United States immigrant from a Central American country. Though speaking Spanish has always been important to her adopted family, Milly pretends she can't understand when Pablo asks her, "¿De dónde eres?" The question leaves Milly with a number of questions of her own about her heritage and her birth parents.

How the Garcia Girls Lost Their Accents by Julia Alvarez, Algonquin, 1991

The 15 interrelated stories that make up the book describe the events surrounding the Garcia's exile from the Dominican Republic. They settle in New York.

How Tia Lola Came to Visit/Stay by Julia Alvarez, Alfred A. Knopf, 2001

Tia Lola is coming from the Dominican Republic to Vermont to visit Miguel, his sister, Juanita, and his mother, but she doesn't speak English, and she refuses to learn. Hoping her visit to the United States will soon be over, Miguel makes Tia Lola a secret he has to keep from his schoolmates. But Tia Lola turns out to be exactly what he needs to keep his mind off his parents' divorce.

Navajo: Visions and Voices Across the Mesa by Shonto Begay, Scholastic, 1995

This collection, which explores Navajo life, pairs Navajo artist Shonto Begay's original poetry with twenty of his paintings. An introduction briefly describes Begay's experiences in a government boarding school where he and the other Navajo children were punished for speaking their native language. The book calls for discussions of how language connects people to their heritage and to those they love.

Cool Salsa: Bilingual Poems on Growing Up Hispanic in the United States edited by Lori M. Carlson, Henry Holt, 1994

In this poetry collection, writers such as Sandra Cisneros, Gary Soto, Ed Vega, and Ana Castillo contribute over 30 poems written in diverse forms about growing up Latina/o. Many of the poems are written in English and include some Spanish words while others have been translated by the editor.

Red Hot Salsa: Bilingual Poems on Being Young and Latino in the United States edited by Lori M. Carlson, Henry Holt, 2005

A companion to *Cool Salsa*, this book also features bilingual poetry about Latinos developing cultural identity within the United States.

Marisol and Magdalena: The Sound of Our Sisterhood by Veronica Chambers, Hyperion, 1998

Marisol and Magdalena fear their friendship will not endure Marisol's year-long stay in Panama with her abuelita. Marisol's life does change during the trip, but the girls remain friends.

Shanghai Messenger by Andrea Cheng, illustrated by Ed Young, Lee & Low, 2005

Grandma Nai Nai sends 11-year-old Xiao Mei from Ohio to Shanghai to meet her extended family and to return to her with "a little bit of China." Xiao Mei worries that her Chinese relatives will not accept her because she is biracial and Grandma Nai Nai has not taught her to speak Chinese. The family embraces Xiao Mei immediately, teaching her important aspects of her family's history as well as Chinese words and phrases. Young's shadowy illustrations accompany each of the free-verse poems, creating a warm book about love, family, and heritage.

Naming Maya by Uma Krishnaswami, Farrar, Straus and Giroux, 2004

A visit from New Jersey to Chennai, India with her mother brings Maya closer to her family heritage. It also brings her closer to understanding that she had nothing to do with her parent's divorce.

A Step from Heaven by An Na, Boyds Mills Press, 2001

At age four, Young Ju and her family move from Korea to America, where they are met with serious challenges, including learning to speak English, combating poverty, and enduring various types of abuse. Particularly interesting to teachers is Young Ju's sense of responsibility for teaching her parents the English words she learns at school.

The Good Rainbow Road by Simon J. Ortiz, illustrated by Michael Lacapa, translated by Victor Montejo, University of Arizona Press, 2004

This trilingual (Spanish, English, and the Native American language, Keres) book is set in Happaahnitse, Oak Place, a village suffering from severe drought. Two brothers, Tsaiyah-dzehshi - First One and Hamahshu-dzehshi - Next One, are asked to travel to Shiwana, the spirits of rain and snow, to ask them to return to the village.

Tangled Threads: A Hmong Girl's Story by Pegi Deitz Shea, Houghton Mifflin, 2003

Thirteen-year-old Mai Yang has lived in Ban Vinai, Thailand, refugee camp, for 10 years before she and her grandmother are finally chosen to go to America to live in Rhode Island with family members. Though life in the United States is more promising than in the refugee camp, Mai and her grandmother find adapting to American culture challenging.

Blue Jasmine by Kashmira Sheth, Hyperion, 2004

Seema is disappointed when she has to move from India to Iowa City, Iowa, with her family where she has to learn a new language and culture. In time, Seema adjusts and learns to like her new life in the United States.

Neighborhood Odes by Gary Soto, illustrated by David Diaz, Harcourt, 1992

Twenty-one poems including Spanish and English words express the significance of little things from eating tortillas and ice cream to riding a bike on a bright, warm day or playing in the sprinklers. The action of the poems could take place in any neighborhood.

Wachale! Poetry and Prose About Growing Up Latino in America edited by Ilan Stavans, Cricket Books, 2001

A bilingual anthology filled with poetry and stories by popular Latino/a authors such as Pat Mora and Gary Soto.

Works Cited

United States Census Bureau Reports. Retrieved September 10, 2006, from http://www.census.gov/prod/2004pubs/p20-551.pdf

Winik, L. W. (2006, August 27). Good schools can happen. *Parade Magazine*. Retrieved October 17, 2006, from http://www.parade.com/articles/editions/2006/edition_08-27-2006/Better_Schools

Chapter *10*

Putting It All Together

M any teachers, scholars and researchers seem to agree that literature, picture books and novels, should be an important feature within content area classrooms as it often serves as a needed complement to dull and difficult textbook chapters. Researchers such as Vacca & Vacca (2005) argue that young adult literature provides depth to topics, such as the Holocaust and slavery, scarcely covered in textbooks. Books such as *I, Dred Scott*, include characters students can come to care about, empathize with, and learn from. Yet, there are other benefits as well. Picture books and young adult novels are often high-interest texts, a welcomed feature when teaching reluctant and illiterate students who need to be motivated before attempting a reading assignment. Some titles (i.e., *The First Part Last* and *Fat Kid Rules the World*) feature youth who have experiences of interest to middle and high school students.

Some of the books in this chapter can be used to encourage discussions and writing assignments about themes and concepts important in content area subjects while others will make excellent read-aloud selections to complement the study of a particular era in social studies and history classes. These books can also help activate prior knowledge, arouse curiosity, and reinforce information found in textbooks.

Awards & Book Lists for Content Area Books

Awards

Carter G. Woodson Award for Children's and Young Adult Literature that depicts ethnicity in the social sciences
http://midhudson.org/Awards/woodson.htm

Notable Social Studies Books for Young People for noteworthy books
www.socialstudies.org/resources/notable

Outstanding Science Trade Books for Students K-12 for quality science trade books
http://www.nsta.org/ostbc

Book Lists

Appraisal: Children's Science Books for Young People, published by Children's Science Book Review Committee

Notable Children's Trade Books in the Field of Social Studies, published annually in *Social Education*

Integrating Multicultural Texts

A Movie in My Pillow/Una Pelicula en Mi Almohada by Jorge Argueta, illustrated by Elizabeth Gómez, Children's Book Press, 2001

In this bilingual picture book, Jorgito and his father flee the war in El Salvador, settling in San Francisco's Mission District. The sights and sounds of the district come alive in the illustrations and language.

Suggestions for Classroom Use

 Read Alike

If you like *Bat 6* (Scholastic, 1998) by Virginia Euwer Wolff, try *Farewell to Manzanar: A True Story of Japanese American Experience During and After the World War II Internment* (Houghton Mifflin, 1973) by Jeanne Wakatsuki Houston and James D. Houston or *Baseball Saved Us* (Lee & Low, 1993) by Ken Mochizuki.

1. This book includes concrete poetry. The words in concrete poems generally take the shape, creating a picture, of the subject of the poem. Using computer software, create a concrete poem about an activity you enjoy doing.

2. What adversities does the protagonist face upon arriving in the United States? How does he overcome them?

3. Using a research source, find out about the civil war in El Salvador during the 1980s/1990s. What was life like for citizens of El Salvador?

4. There is poetic language throughout this book. Go on a figurative language hunt. How many metaphors and similes can you identify?

5. Compare and contrast life for Jorgito in El Salvador and San Francisco.

6. Locate El Salvador on a map. What surrounds it? How far is it from the United States?

Hidden Roots by Joseph Bruchac, Scholastic, 2004

Sonny is stunned when he learns his family has Native American heritage and that Uncle Louis is really his maternal grandfather. Environmental issues and the historical setting add depth to the novel.

Suggestions for Classroom Use

1. Create a discussion web (Vacca & Vacca, 2005) by drawing a line down the middle of a sheet of paper. On one side of the line write YES. On the other side of the line write NO. In the white space at the top of the page, write the following question: Should the protagonists' parents have embraced their Native American heritage? On the side where you have written YES, list 3-5 reasons why his parents should have embraced their Native American heritage. On the side where you have written NO, list 3-5 reasons why his parents should not have embraced their Native American heritage. After discussing your reasons with classmates, decide if you would answer the question affirmatively or negatively and explain why in a corner at the bottom of the page.

 Read Alike

If you like *Coolies* (Penguin, 2001) by Yin, try *Dragonwings* (Harper, 1975) and *Dragon's Gate* (HarperCollins, 1993) by Laurence Yep.

2. When chemicals from the plant pollute the river, why does the water look multicolored?

3. Using resources, find out when Vermont was established. Who were some of the early settlers? Which Native American tribes made their homes there?

4. List the stereotypes Sonny has learned about Native Americans. Which books does the librarian give to him? Find out what the books are about? Do you think these books will help Sonny dispel some of the stereotypes he has learned about Native Americans?

5. Based on the information Sonny gives, what was life like in the United States shortly after the Korean War? Who was president?

6. Do research to find out about Hurricane Carol of 1954. Find out its origins, level and areas of impact, and storm path in the United States.

7. Read Nancy L. Gallagher's *Breeding Better Vermonters: The Eugenics Project in the Green Mountain State* (University Press of New England, 1999) to learn more about that.

The First Part Last by Angela Johnson, Simon & Schuster, 2003

In this award-winning prequel to *Heaven*, 16-year-old Bobby takes on the responsibility of raising his daughter, Feather. Though it isn't easy, Bobby leaves New York and the support of his family and moves to Ohio with his daughter.

Suggestions for Classroom Use

1. Using resources in the library, learn more about teen pregnancy, teen parenting, and adoption.
2. Visit <http://www.preeclampsia.org> to learn more about preeclampsia.
3. Inspired by the art of graffiti, create a picture that expresses the theme of this book. What do you think the author's message is?
4. Reread Bobby's fairy tale about his life. Draft a fairy tale of your own about your life.
5. If you would like to learn more about the author, read *Angela Johnson: Poetic Prose* (Rowman & Littlefield, 2006).
6. Write an obituary for Nia.
7. Write a new ending for the book that describes what happens when Bobby decides to give Feather up for adoption.

Select Awards & Honors

Coretta Scott King Award
Michael L. Printz Award

Online Multicultural Resources

Evaluating and Selecting Multicultural Literature

http://www.4children.org/news/9-97mlit.htm and/or
http://ecrp.uiuc.edu/v3n2/mendoza.html
http://teacher.scholastic.com/products/instructor/multicultural.htm

---

Carver: A Life in Poems by Marilyn Nelson, Boyd Mills, 1997

Over 40 poems chronicle the life and work of botanist and inventor, Dr. George Washington Carver. Dr. Carver invented numerous uses for the peanut. He served as a professor at Tuskegee Institute, now called Tuskegee University.

Suggestions for Classroom Use

1. Visit <http://www.lib.iastate.edu/spcl/gwc/home.html> to learn more about Dr. Carver and to see photos and browse other resources about him.

2. Visit <http://www.lib.iastate.edu/spcl/gwc/resources/furtherresearch. html> to read peanut recipes and other uses of the peanut and the sweet potato endorsed by Dr. Carver.

3. Keep an About-Point (Manzo, Manzo, & Estes, 2001) Log. After reading each poem, write down its title and complete the following sentence: This poem is about _____; and the point is_____.
While reading, keep a chart of Dr. Carver's scientific contributions.

4. Using a research source, find out more about the Tuskegee Airmen. You might also be interested in the film, *The Tuskegee Airmen* (HBO Films, 1995), directed by Robert Markowitz.

Select Awards & Honors

John Newbery Honor Award
Coretta Scott King Honor Award

When the Levees Broke: A Requiem in Four Acts directed by Spike Lee, HBO, 2006

This film is a documentary describing citizens of the Gulf Coast, the United States president, governmental officers and organizations' response to hurricane warnings and the devastation of the Gulf Coast. The documentary suggests that the government should have done a better job of helping citizens get to safety.

Suggestions for Classroom Use

1. After viewing the documentary, fill out a Who-What-When-Where-How Outline (Manzo, Manzo, & Estes, 2001).

2. Play the Questions Game (Allen, 2004) with classmates. After viewing the documentary, write down at least three questions about things you would like to know more about or found difficult to understand. Exchange your list of questions with someone else. While your partner is answering your questions, you must answer her questions. Then discuss the questions and possible answers together. Do any new questions emerge? If so, seek additional answers, including additional classmates in your group if possible.

3. Visit <http://en.wikipedia.org/wiki/When_the_Levees_Broke> for a synopsis of the documentary and a list of those interviewed. According to the documentary, why *did* the levees break? What evidence exists to support this theory?

4. Visit <http://www.npr.org/templates/story/story.php?storyId=5200940> to read a timeline of events leading up to the hurricane's arrival. What was the local government's response? The U.S. government's response?

5. Do research to find out about Hurricane Betsy of 1965. Find out its origins, level, and areas of impact in the United States, particularly in Louisiana.

6. Choose one of the people interviewed in the documentary and create a dialogue between that individual and President Bush.

7. Some people compare the effects of Hurricane Katrina with the Mississippi River Flood of 1927. Research and compare the similarities and differences between these two effects.

8. With classmates, put FEMA, government officials, and citizens of the gulf coast on trial. Who was responsible for the adversity surrounding the hurricane and to what degree?

Additional Titles

The Birchbark House by Louise Erdrich, Hyperion, 1999

Set during the 1800s, Omakayas, or Little Frog, and her Ojibwa family live and work on Lake Superior. The community is a peaceful one until a man brings smallpox to the citizens.

Fat Kid Rules the World by K.L. Going, Penguin, 2003

Overweight, suicidal protagonist, Troy, joins forces with thin, drug addicted Kurt, to form a rock group. Kurt helps Troy develop self-esteem while Troy helps him overcome his drug problem.

Out of the Dust by Karen Hesse, Scholastic, 1997

Written in free verse and set in the 1930s, Billie Jo and her family struggle to make a living during the depression and the dust bowl. When Billie Jo's mother and her unborn sibling die, Billie Jo's life is completely changed.

Still I Rise: A Cartoon History of African Americans by Roland Owen Laird and Taneshia Laird, illustrated by Elihu Bey, W.W. Norton, 1997

This graphic novel includes the contributions of African Americans in science, art, education, space exploration, and more. The book focuses on the accomplishments of African Americans from the 17th century when African Americans entered the United States as indentured servants to the 1990s.

Looking for Alibrandi by Melina Marchetta, Orchard, 1999

Born in Australia, Josie Alibrandi, an illegitimate child of a single mother in a strong-willed Italian Catholic extended family, develops a relationship with her birth father. Facing her own awakening sexuality, she struggles with memories of the ostracism and prejudices her mother faced. *Looking for Alibrandi* was a major Australian film released in 2000.

I, Dred Scott: A Fictional Slave Narrative Based on the Life and Legal Precedent of Dred Scott by Sheila P. Moses, Simon & Schuster, 2005

Engaged in a legal battle for his family's freedom, Dred Scott's lawyers argued that he and his wife should be granted freedom since their owners took them into free states. Despite the Missouri Compromise, the Supreme Court ruling argued that slaves were not citizens of the United States.

Patrol: An American Soldier in Vietnam by Walter Dean Myers, HarperCollins, 2002

Wartime is depicted as an American soldier does his job under adverse and frightening conditions, revealing the difficult task of fighting for one's country. Though set during the Vietnam War, parallels can also be made to Desert Storm or the war in Iraq.

Project Mulberry: A Novel by Linda Sue Park, Clarion Books, 2005

Julia Song wonders about racism, prejudice, and assimilation while she and her friend Patrick raise silkworms for their agricultural club project and learn about self-sustained farming. The discussion between the author and her main character in alternate chapters reveal Park's writing process.

Esperanza Rising by Pam Munoz Ryan, Scholastic, 2001

Set during the United States depression of the 1930s, Esperanza's life of wealth and luxury comes to an abrupt end when her father dies. She and her mother immigrate to the United States, joining their former servants as migrant workers in California.

Milkweed by Jerry Spinelli, Random House, 2003

An orphan is given the name Misha Pilsudski and a gypsy heritage by an orphan boy named Uri who tries to protect him from Nazis in Poland. Surviving destitution and horrific living conditions, Misha matures, becomes an adult, and moves to the United States where he commits himself to telling everyone about his experiences.

The Black Brothers by Lisa Tetzner, illustrated by Hannes Binder, Boyds Mills Press, 2004

This graphic novel depicts the plight of poverty stricken chimney sweepers in Italy. The main character, Giorgio, manages to obtain support from a gang of boys like himself before fleeing adverse conditions.

Bat 6 by Virginia Euwer Wolff, Scholastic, 1998

Set in Oregon during the 1940s, multiple narrators describe events around an annual sixth grade baseball game. Conflict arises when events that occurred during World War II causes one of the girls to hate another one because she is Japanese.

Behind the Wheel: Poems About Driving by Janet Wong, Margaret K. McElderry, 1999

In this collection, driving is presented metaphorically. The free verse poems include multiple voices that explore what it means to learn to become a responsible driver and a responsible person.

Coolies by Yin, illustrated by Chris K. Soentpiet, Penguin, 2001

A boy's grandmother tells him about the difficulties faced by his ancestors when they immigrated to the United States in 1865 to help build the transcontinental railroads. They endured injustices and dangerous working conditions.

Briar Rose by Jane Yolen, Tor Books, 1992

Rebecca faintly recalls the story of Sleeping Beauty told to her by her grandmother, who is now dying. The story encourages her to learn more about her grandmother's life, uncovering her past in Poland during the Holocaust.

Works Cited

Allen, J. (2004), *Tools for Teaching Content Literacy*. Portland, Maine: Stenhouse.

Hinton, K. (2006). *Angela Johnson: Poetic prose*. Lanham, Maryland: Rowman & Littlefield.

Vacca, R. T., & Vacca, J. A. (2005). *Content area reading: Literacy and learning across the curriculum*. Boston: Pearson.

Collaboration Ideas

Interdisciplinary

An interdisciplinary approach is hardest to achieve with the core academic subjects of math, science, language arts, and social studies, at least from the teacher perspective. From the student perspective, many of the elements that they study are intertwined. In science, they learn about volcanoes, but at the same time they are learning about ancient Pompeii in social studies. The core academic subjects are not the only areas for interdisciplinary or multidisciplinary work. Family and consumer science classes have a wealth of opportunities, as well as foreign language, technology, and other electives. This group of collaboration ideas is organized around opportunities for collaboration.

Language Arts

What is the science in science fiction? Students will read a science fiction novel, and then explain the scientific concepts in each. Students will present their findings in science fair format.

What is the science in fantasy? Fantastic fiction is beyond the realm of science, but students can investigate exactly why the concepts presented cannot happen, i.e., why humans cannot fly, why birds cannot talk, etc.

Foreign Language

Pairing with social studies classes, students create dialogues to reenact scenes of historical importance. For instance, the scene between Christopher Columbus and Queen Isabella of Spain; between Napoleon and his troops, important battles with Germany and Japan in World War II, and other language-specific situations. This can test the student's knowledge of the events and the student's grasp of the language.

Taking the part of an immigrant seeking U.S. citizenship, students work to prepare a study guide on U.S. history and the Constitution in the native language of the immigrant.

Math

Students use inflation calculators to understand the costs of goods and services aligned with wages by bringing the costs to current levels.

Students read novels such as *The Da Vinci Code* (Doubleday, 2003) by Dan Brown in which math puzzles were part of the plot. Students propose other ideas for novels using math concepts.

Career Studies

In most states, subject classroom teachers are expected to teach students about the opportunities for careers in that field. To make this opportunity a more interdisciplinary learning opportunity, ask students to research a particular person, then develop a lesson teaching the important points of his or her life work. Presentation would be the content lesson taught by Dr. Einstein, Madame Curie, and George Washington Carver. This could be a good review tool at the end of the semester.

Chapter *11*

Popular Culture

A group of librarians on an online discussion list were talking about adding materials to the library collection to aid students in playing and defeating video games. Although there were some pros and cons in terms of which games should be considered or which were too violent or too juvenile, it was generally decided that adding the video game assistance materials was a good thing. The materials would aid in encouraging young adults to read and it would show them that the school library is a natural place to find information to meet their needs.

Reluctantly, another librarian joined in the discussion and said that she had talked this over with numerous teens at her high school library. To her surprise, she could find no one who played video games on a regular basis. The students were fairly harsh on their descriptions of those who spent time in this manner, ranging from "babies," i.e., "we did that in middle school," to "losers," as in, "we have other things to spend time on now." When she posted this, rather tentatively, more librarians joined in citing similar responses from youth.

So another stereotype became shattered, and we learned that not all young adults in high school spend their time playing video games. In some high schools, almost no one does. That fact was startling in its simplicity to the librarians on the discussion list, but it highlights the dangers of blanketing an entire age group with a stereotype drawn from television, movies, or magazines. Even our own memories can be faulty. What parent has not planned an activity or bought clothing for a teen that seemed to be perfect and completely in style only to be told, "Mom, no one wears that anymore."

Popular culture is loosely defined as the mass of media, impressions, stereotypes, and influences that surround us in daily life. Those who study pop culture are intrigued by the way our lives interact with these influences, from the way the latest television commercial jingle becomes part of the lexicon of life, to the images of music videos or movies that are seen as icons for the current age. The strongest influences today are probably seen as the entertainment industries, especially music and television. However, popular culture existed long before electronic media. Songs, stories, games, and poems have always created a temporary escape from mundane life.

Just like today, the popular culture influences on the youth of hundreds of years ago most likely disturbed the adults of those eras. There is no doubt that the teenager presented through the lens of popular culture has always been disturbing to parents and other adults.

In Oliker and Krolikowski's (2001) book on how popular culture influences and educates teens, they designed the book cover to illustrate the relationships between adults, youth, and media. On that cover, a group of three youth (James Dean, Elvis, and teen blonde bombshell Marie Windsor) are seen on television. Watching television are three youths who have adopted the dress and mannerisms of James Dean, Elvis, and Marie Windsor. Watching this phenomenon are two adults. The first is noted educational philosopher John Dewey, who looks at the scene with obvious dismay and sadness. The other adult is Superman, who consoles John Dewey while watching the scene with a look that could be either satisfaction with the scene or confidence in the ability of Superman to transcend negative images to become a true teen model.

Thus, in Oliker and Krolikowski's view, the teens become the virtual mirror image of what they watch on television. Other voices, such as Bill Osgerby (2004) in his work *Youth Media*, see the link as more of an exchange. Media work to portray teens in a specific story or advertisement, which then influences all youth. The teens dress or act more like their portrayals in music, film, and television, thus providing more images of teens from which the media can draw to make more portrayals.

The portrayals of teens in books follow this same view. Hollis Woods is no more the typical foster child than Gilly Hopkins was for the previous generation. Lipsyte's *The Contender* (Harper, 1967) and Crutcher's *Whale Talk* (Greenwillow, 2001) both portray athletes whose personal lives are the focus of much of the novels, but they are decades apart.

In selecting materials for young adults, the pop culture stereotypes must be taken into consideration as well. In truth, not every rural teen loves country music. Not every urban teen listens to hip-hop. Not every girl reads romance stories. Not every boy yearns to have his own set of wheels. As much as the popular culture world tries to present a single one-sided view of each generation, the struggle for individuality will always win. Sometimes this can be surprising.

Studying Popular Culture

One way to encourage young adults to look past the stereotypes that are presented to them on a daily basis is to have them use pop culture as a research tool. Current topics such as the fast food industry as a factor in the obesity of Americans, the increasing interest in plastic surgery for teens, or the way that business uses social networking tools such as <myspace.com> to advertise their products are fascinating for teens.

Economics or business classes can use pop culture companies to investigate the stock market, or to watch a new product enter the market. Today teens have short memories, and a teacher may think it is cool to bring in companies that have risen and fallen such as Napster, only to have students say, "What's Napster?" Four years is a generation for high school students.

Works Cited

Crutcher, C. (2001). *Whale Talk*, New York: Greenwillow.

Giff, P. R. (2002). *Pictures of Hollis Woods*. New York: Random House.

Lipsyte, R. (1967). *The Contender.* New York: Harper.

Oliker, M. A., & Krolikowski, W. P. (Eds.). (2001). *Images of youth: Popular culture as educational ideology.* New York: Peter Lang.

Osgerby, B. (2004). *Youth media.* New York: Taylor & Francis.

Patterson, K. (1978). *The Great Gilly Hopkins.* New York: HarperCollins.

Chapter *12*

Advocating Multiculturalism

The first semester of college can be a learning experience in many ways. Nowhere is the learning experience more intense than learning to get along with a roommate. Many high school teens have never shared a room in their entire lives, and some are the only child in the household. Living in close quarters has always been a difficult adjustment. Elizabeth Farrell (2006), in her article in the *Chronicle of Higher Education*, adds a new twist to the parental anxiety scale by noting the use of Facebook and Myspace in making stereotypical judgments about their child's prospective roommate.

Farrell did research for her article with residential life directors from a variety of colleges and found that parents were making assumptions about their child's prospective roommate based on the roommate's Myspace or Facebook page. They read between the lines of the page to find hints of drug or alcohol use, of being too preppy or too gothic, and of being too poor or too rich. The directors, when they received frantic calls from parents, always suggested that it would be best for the two freshmen to actually meet and try living together before deciding that sharing a room would be impossible. The directors also checked the links parents provided and could find no evidence of such activity. Parents were making the assumptions based on the prospective roommate's photos, music choices, or language.

Farrell's (2006) work provides an opportunity for working with parents to encourage a wider view of multiculturalism. As noted in Chapter 11, the media presents teens in extremely stereotypical ways. Reading the newspaper about teen crimes in other cities or viewing teen-oriented movies and television programs do little to combat stereotypes.

It is best to work with parents bombarded by stereotypical images of young adults in two ways: first, by encouraging parents to present multicultural literature to students at a young age, and second, by reading multicultural literature that presents a non-stereotypical view of youth themselves. Pauletta Brown Bracy (2006) offers clear criteria to parents and teachers interested in advocating for multicultural literature at home and at school:

- **Classrooms Are Diverse Settings**
  Our children's classrooms are part of their world, not ours. They play, work, and live for a major part of each day with other young people. The books that parents read with their children can be a bond between parent and child. Reading books with multicultural characters together helps to create that bond.

- **Literary Criteria and Multicultural Literature**
  Multicultural books should meet the same literary criteria as all other literature. Hey, Look! We're Multicultural! may scream from the latest publisher's display rack at conferences, but using the same selection criteria to evaluate multicultural books that are applied to all literature and other resources shows a respect for these genres. Selecting books based on literary merit, accuracy, relationship to the curriculum, and overall value in terms of leisure reading interests and informational reading needs of students and teachers is key to true integration of literature.

- **Criticism**
  Bracy (2006) points out that multicultural literature is especially vulnerable to criticism that focuses on bias, stereotyping, and misinformation. Multicultural literature may also become quickly dated as societal values change. Weeding outdated literature and other resources is crucial to the success of a strong multicultural literature program.

- **Positive Imagery**
  Positive imagery is imperative. It is not enough to have resources that are merely free from bias or stereotypes. A more difficult task is to find resources that portray a positive image. Popular culture depicts people of color excelling in entertainment or sports, as if this is the extent of their accomplishments. Conversely, whites are depicted as successful at a myriad of careers. It is rarer to find resources that portray, both directly through focused text and indirectly through visuals, minorities in roles common to everyday life.

- **Accuracy**
  Accurate narratives are non-negotiable. There are those that claim that in order to be truly authentic, an author needs to be from that culture. In other words, an author writing about the Native American experience should be Native American; those writing about different cultural experiences should have had those experiences. Others claim that writers, good writers, can reach into the soul of others and write from that insight,

write from imagination. Regardless of which viewpoint the narrative is written, it should honestly represent the multicultural experience.

- **Mirrors or Windows**

  Multicultural books serve as mirrors or windows. Especially important to parents, Bracy (2006) shows the true importance of using multicultural literature. It can reflect the child's experiences and can illustrate the experiences of others. There are no generic books. A multiculturally rich collection of resources will contain many windows and mirrors. No one or two resources truly capture the rich experiences of a multicultural society. Providing one or two examples of a culture is more likely to raise the point described before in presenting a stereotype or bias of a culture.

- **Affirmation**

  If you can't affirm, don't confirm. This point speaks to weeding the collection frequently. It is difficult at times to search for resources that fit the previous points and add value to the library, classroom, or home collection. Negative images should be removed, regardless of age or ability to be replaced. Simple announcements about the context of the times or a written note at the beginning of a resource noting that it contains stereotypes or bias are unacceptable. There is an old adage "you can't talk yourself out of situations you behaved yourself into." Allowing materials to present non-affirming images only confirms a behavior that cannot be tolerated. No amount of talking will undo this.

Summary

Advocating for multicultural materials in libraries, classroom, and home collections at the secondary level is a combination of teaching, modeling, and seeking constant opportunities. Our students see the multicultural world around them, but they may not visualize the world of resources and information as being integrated into their academic life. Teachers and parents should seize and welcome opportunities to advocate for multicultural resources.

Works Cited

Bracy, P. B. (2006). Examining multicultural literature: Making a commitment, meeting a demand in diverse cultural classrooms. *First Read*, 2(4), 4-5.

Farrell, E. (Sept 1, 2006). Judging roommates by their facebook cover. *Chronicle of Higher Education*, 53(2), A63-A64.

Appendix A: Young Adult Title List by Author's Last Name

Navajo Code Talkers
by Nathan Aaseng
Walker, 1992

Finding Miracles
by Julia Alvarez
Alfred A. Knopf, 2004

How The Garcia Girls Lost Their Accents
by Julia Alvarez
Algonquin, 1991

How Tia Lola Came to Visit/Stay
by Julia Alvarez
Alfred A. Knopf, 2001

Bless Me, Ultima
by Rudolfo Anaya
Quinto Sol, 1972

Elegy on the Death of Cesar Chavez: A Poem
by Rudolfo Anaya
illustrated by Gaspar Enriquez
Cinco Puntos, 2000

A Movie in My Pillow/Una Pelicula en Mi Almohada
by Jorge Argueta
illustrated by Elizabeth Gómez
Children's Book Press, 2001

Dude! Stories and Stuff for Boys
edited by Sandy Asher and David L. Harrison
Penguin, 2006

On Her Way: Stories and Poems About Growing Up a Girl
edited by Sandy Asher
Penguin, 2004

With All My Heart, With All My Mind: Thirteen Stories About Growing Up Jewish
edited by Sandy Asher
Simon & Schuster, 1999

Am I Blue?: Coming Out from the Silence
edited by Marion Dane Bauer
HarperCollins, 1994

Navajo: Visions and Voices Across the Mesa
by Shonto Begay
Scholastic, 1995

Cesar: ¡Sí, Se Puede! (Yes, We Can!)
by Carmen T. Bernier-Grand
illustrated by David Diaz
Marshall Cavendish, 2004

Rock of Ages: A Tribute to the Black Church
by Tonya Bolden
illustrated by R. Gregory Christie
Random House, 2001

Between Earth & Sky: Legends of Native American Sacred Places
by Joseph Bruchac
illustrated by Thomas Locker
Harcourt, 1996

Code Talker: A Novel About the Navajo Marines of World War Two
by Joseph Bruchac
Dial, 2005

Hidden Roots
by Joseph Bruchac
Scholastic, 2004

The Heart of a Chief
by Joseph Bruchac
Dial, 1998

The Tequila Worm
by Viola Canales
Random House, 2005

Real Women Have Curves
Rating: PG 13
directed by Patricia Cardoso
screenplay by George Lavoo and
Josefina Lopez
HBO Films, 2002
Select Awards & Honors: Audience
Award at Sundance Film Festival 2002

*American Eyes: New Asian-American
Short Stories for Young Adults*
edited by Lori Marie Carlson
Henry Holt & Company, 1994

*Cool Salsa: Bilingual Poems
on Growing Up Hispanic in
the United States*
edited by Lori M. Carlson
Henry Holt, 1994

*Moccasin Thunder: American Indian
Stories for Today*
edited by Lori Marie Carlson
HarperCollins, 2005

*Red Hot Salsa: Bilingual Poems
on Being Young and Latino in the
United States*
edited by Lori M. Carlson
Henry Holt, 2005

Love and Sex: Ten Stories of Truth
edited by Michael Cart
Simon & Schuster, 2001

Who Will Tell My Brother?
by Marlene Carvell
Hyperion, 2002

*Marisol and Magdalena: The Sound
of Our Sisterhood*
by Veronica Chambers
Hyperion, 1998

Quinceañera Means Sweet 15
by Veronica Chambers
Hyperion, 2001

Shanghai Messenger
by Andrea Cheng
illustrated by Ed Young
Lee & Low, 2005

The House on Mango Street
by Sandra Cisneros
Arte Publico, 1984

Growing Up Poor: A Literary Anthology
edited by Robert Coles and Randy
Testa with Michael Coles
New Press, 2001

Burning Up
by Caroline B. Cooney
Delacorte, 1999

Walk Two Moons
by Sharon Creech
HarperCollins, 1994

Whale Talk
by Chris Crutcher
Greenwillow, 2001

Bucking the Sarge
by Christopher Paul Curtis
Random House, 2004

*The Heart Knows Something Different:
Teenage Voices from the Foster Care
System: Youth Communication*
edited by Al Desetta
Persea Books, 1996

A Yellow Raft in Blue Water
by Michael Dorris
Henry Holt & Company, 1987

Copper Sun
by Sharon Draper
Simon & Schuster, 2006

*Unsung Heros of World War II: The
Story of the Navajo Code Talkers*
by Deanne Durrett
Facts on File, 1998

The Birchbark House
by Louise Erdrich
Hyperion, 1999

Love Medicine
by Louise Erdrich
Holt, 1984

Party Girl
by Lynne Ewing
Alfred Knopf, 1998

Finding Fish: A Memoir
by Antwone Quenton Fisher, Mim
Eichler Rivas
Morrow, 2001

Bang!
by Sharon Flake
Hyperion, 2005

Seedfolks
by Paul Fleischman
HarperCollins, 1997

Crossing Jordan
by Adrian Fogelin
Peachtree, 2000

*Things I Have to Tell You: Poems
and Writing by Teenage Girls*
edited by Betsy Franco
photographs by Nina Nickles
Candlewick, 2001

*You Hear Me?: Poems and Writing
by Teenage Boys*
edited by Betsy Franco
photographs by Nina Nickles
Candlewick, 2000

Keesha's House
by Helen Frost
Farrar, Straus and Giroux, 2003

Spinning Through the Universe
by Helen Frost
Frances Foster, 2004

*Breeding Better Vermonters:
The Eugenics Project in the
Green Mountain State*
by Nancy L. Gallagher
University Press of New England, 1999

*First Crossing: Stories About Teen
Immigrants*
by Donald R. Gallo
Candlewick Press, 2004

Annie On My Mind
by Nancy Garden
Farrar, Straus and Giroux, 1982

Maggie's Door
by Patricia Reilly Giff
Random House, 2003

Pictures of Hollis Wood
by Patricia Reilly Giff
Random House, 2002
Select Awards & Honors: Newbery
Honor 2003, ALA Best Books for
Young Adults 2003, ALA Notable
Children's Books 2003

Fat Kid Rules the World
by K. L. Going
Penguin, 2003

Dark Sons
by Nikki Grimes
Hyperion, 2005

*The Curious Incident of the Dog in
the Night-time*
by Mark Haddon
Doubleday, 2003

*Cinnamon Girl: Letters Found Inside
a Cereal Box*
by Juan Felipe Herrera
Joanna Cotler, 2005

Aleutian Sparrow
by Karen Hesse
Margaret K. McElderry, 2003

Letters from Rifka
by Karen Hesse
Henry Holt, 1992
Select Awards & Honors: National
Jewish Book Award, Sydney Taylor
Book Award, Christopher Book Award

Out of the Dust
by Karen Hesse
Scholastic, 1997

Witness
by Karen Hesse
Scholastic Press, 2001

*Fishing for Chickens: Short Stories
About Rural Youth*
edited by Jim Heynen
Persea, 2001

Susannah
by Janet Hickman
Greenwillow Books, 1998

Born Confused
by Tanuja Desai Hidier
Scholastic, 2002

Angela Johnson: Poetic Prose
by KaaVonia Hinton
Rowman & Littlefield, 2006

Rising Voices: Writings of Young Native Americans
edited by Arlene Hirschfelder and Beverly R. Singer
Simon & Schuster, 1992

Farewll to Manzanar: A True Story of Japanese American Experience During and After the World War II Internment
by Jeanne Wakatsuki Houston and James D. Houston
Houghton Mifflin, 1973

Breaking Through
by Francisco Jiménez
Houghton Mifflin, 2001

The Curcuit: Stories from the Life of a Migrant Child
by Francisco Jiménez
University of New Mexico Press, 1997

La Mariposa
by Francisco Jiménez
Houghton Mifflin, 1998

The First Part Last
by Angela Johnson
Simon & Schuster, 2003
Select Awards & Honors: Coretta Scott King Award, Michael L. Printz Award

Heaven
by Angela Johnson
Simon & Schuster, 1998

Soul Moon Soup
by Lindsay Lee Johnson
Boyds Mills, 1998

The Known World
by Edward P. Jones
Amistad, 2003

Kira-Kira
by Cynthia Kadohata
Simon & Schuster, 2004
Select Awards & Honors: John Newbery Medal, Asian/Pacific American Award for Literature

Warriors: Navajo Code Talkers
by Kenji Kawano
Northland Pub. Co, 1990

Deliver Us from Evie
by M.E. Kerr
HarperCollins, 1994

The Secret Life of Bees
by Sue Monk Kidd
Viking, 2002

Quinceañera: Celebrating Fifteen
by Elizabeth King
Dutton, 1998

The Woman Warrior: Memoirs of a Girlhood Among Ghosts
by Maxine Hong Kingston
Knopf, 1976

The Brimstone Journals
by Ronald Koertge
Candlewick Press, 2001

Spite Fences
by Trudy Krisher
Delacorte, 1994

Naming Maya
by Uma Krishnaswami
Farrar, Straus and Giroux, 2004

Still I Rise: A Cartoon History of African Americans
by Roland Owen Laird and Taneshia Laird
illustrated by Elihu Bey
W.W. Norton, 1997

Native Speaker
by Chang-Rae Lee
Riverhead, 1995

I Once Was a Monkey: Stories Buddha Told
by Jeanne M. Lee
Farrar, Straus and Giroux, 1999

Necessary Roughness
by Marie G. Lee
HarperCollins, 1996

When the Levees Broke: A Requiem in Four Acts
directed by Spike Lee
HBO, 2006

Boy Meets Boy
by David Levithan
Random House, 2003

The Contender
by Robert Lipsyte
Harper, 1967

Confessions of a Closet Catholic
by Sarah Darer Littman
Penguin, 2005

Girls Got Game: Sports Stories and Poems
by Sue Macy
Henry Holt & Company, 2001

Looking for Alibrandi
by Melina Marchetta
Orchard, 1999

The Tuskegee Airmen
directed by Robert Markowitz
HBO Films, 1995

Parrot in the Oven: Mi Vida
by Victor Martinez
HarperCollins, 1996

The Flip Side
by Andrew Matthews
Random House, 2003

My Chinatown
by Kam Max
HarperCollins, 2001

Chill Wind
by Janet McDonald
Farrar, Straus and Giroux, 2002

Twists and Turns
by Janet McDonald
Farrar, Straus and Giroux, 2003

Baseball Saved Us
by Ken Mochizuki
Lee & Low, 1993

Beacon Hill Boys
by Ken Mochizuki
Scholastic, 2002

House Made of Dawn
by N. Scott Momaday
Harper, 1968

The Bluest Eye
by Toni Morrison
Holt, Rinehart, and Winston, 1970

The Baptism
by Sheila P. Moses
Simon & Schuster, 2007

I, Dred Scott: A Fictional Slave Narrative Based on the Life and Legal Precedent of Dred Scott
by Sheila P. Moses
Simon & Schuster, 2005

The Legend of Buddy Bush
by Sheila P. Moses
Margaret K. McElderry, 2003

The Return of Buddy Bush
by Sheila P. Moses
Margaret K. McElderry, 2005

Zen Shorts
by John Muth
Scholastic, 2005

Autobiography of My Dead Brother
by Walter Dean Myers
art by Christopher Myers
HarperCollins, 2005

The Beast
by Walter Dean Myers
Scholastic, 2003

Monster
by Walter Dean Myers
illustrated by Christopher Myers
HarperCollins, 1999

Patrol: An American Soldier in Vietnam
by Walter Dean Myers
HarperCollins, 2002

Shooter
by Walter Dean Myers
HarperCollins, 2004

A Step from Heaven
by An Na
Boyds Mills Press, 2001

Carver: A Life in Poems
by Marilyn Nelson
Boyds Mills, 1997
Select Awards & Honors: John
Newbery Honor Award, Coretta Scott
King Honor Award

Come with Me: Poems for a Journey
by Naomi Shihab Nye
illustrated by Dan Yaccarino
Greenwillow, 2000

Habibi
by Naomi Shihab Nye
Simon & Schuster, 1997

Buddha Book: A Meeting of Images
by Frank Olinksy
Diane Publishing, 1997

The Good Rainbow Road
by Simon J. Ortiz
illustrated by Michael Lacapa
translated by Victor Montejo
University of Arizona Press, 2004

Cuba 15
by Nancy Osa
Random House, 2003
Select Awards & Honors: Pura Belpré
Honor Book, An ALA Notable Book,
An ALA Best Book for Young Adults,
A *Booklist* Top Ten Youth First Novels

When the Emperor Was Divine
by Julie Otsuka
Knopf, 2002

Music from a Place Called Half Moon
by Jerrie Oughton
Houghton Mifflin, 1995

Project Mulberry: A Novel
by Linda Sue Park
Clarion Books, 2005

*The Glass Café or, the Stripper and
the State: How My Mother Started A
War with the System That Made Us
Kind of Rich and a Little Bit Famous*
by Gary Paulsen
Random House, 2003

Nightjohn
by Gary Paulsen
Delacorte, 1993

Keeping You a Secret
by Julie Anne Peters
Little, Brown, Co., 2003

*Mixed: An Anthology of Short Fiction
on the Multiracial Experience*
edited by Chandra Prasad
W.W. Norton, 2006

Yellow Star
by Jennifer Roy
Marshall Cavendish, 2006

Esperanza Rising
by Pam Munoz Ryan
Scholastic, 2001

God Went to Beauty School
by Cynthia Rylant
HarperCollins, 2003

Rainbow Boys
by Alex Sanchez
Simon & Schuster, 2001

Rainbow High
by Alex Sanchez
Simon & Schuster, 2003

Rainbow Road
by Alex Sanchez
Simon & Schuster, 2005

Home of the Brave
by Allen Say
Houghton Mifflin, 2002

Guys Write for Guys Read
edited by Jon Scieszka
Viking Penguin, 2005

Tangled Threads: A Hmong Girl's Story
by Pegi Deitz Shea
Houghton Mifflin, 2003

Blue Jasmine
by Kashmira Sheth
Hyperion, 2004

Ceremony
by Leslie Marmon Silko
Viking, 1977

I Believe in Water: Twelve Brushes with Religion
edited by Marilyn Singer
HarperCollins, 2000

Dust
by Arthur G. Slade
Random House, 2003

Indian Shoes
by Cynthia Leitich Smith
HarperCollins, 2002

Rain Is Not My Indian Name
by Cynthia Leitich Smith
HarperCollins, 2001

The Way a Door Closes
by Hope Anita Smith
illustrations by Shane W. Evans
Henry Holt, 2003

Sparrow
by Sherri L. Smith
Random House, 2006

Buried Onions
by Gary Soto
Harcourt, 1997

Neighborhood Odes
by Gary Soto
illustrated by David Diaz
Harcourt, 1992

Milkweed
by Jerry Spinelli
Random House, 2003

Wachale! Poetry and Prose About Growing Up Latino in America
edited by Ilan Stavans
Cricket Books, 2001

The Journey
by Sarah Stewart
illustrated by David Small
Farrar, Straus and Giroux, 2001

Sacred Places
by Philemon Sturges
illustrated by Giles Laroche
Penguin Young, 2000

The Black Brothers
by Lisa Tetzner
illustrated by Hannes Binder
Boyds Mills Press, 2004

Blankets
by Craig Thompson
Top Shelf, 2003

In Search of Our Mothers' Gardens
by Alice Walker
Harcourt Brace Jovanovich, 1983

Making Up Megaboy
by Virginia Walter
illustrated by Katrina Roeckelein
DK Publishing, 1998

Learning the Game
by Kevin Waltman
Scholastic, 2005

Montana, 1948
by Larry Watson
Milkweed, 1993
Select Awards & Honors: 1993
Milkweed National Fiction Prize

Big City Cool: Short Stories About Urban Youth
edited by M. Jerry Weiss and Helen S. Weiss
Persea, 2002

Like Sisters on the Homefront
by Rita Williams-Garcia
Lodestar, 1995

No Laughter Here
by Rita Williams-Garcia
HarperCollins, 2003

Hard Love
by Ellen Wittlinger
Simon & Schuster, 1999

Bat 6
by Virginia Euwer Wolff
Scholastic, 1998

Make Lemonade
by Virginia Euwer Wolff
Henry Holt, 1993

True Believer
by Virginia Euwer Wolff
Atheneum, 2001

Behind the Wheel: Poems About Driving
by Janet Wong
Margaret K. McElderry, 1999

A Suitcase Full of Seaweed and Other Poems
by Janet S. Wong
Simon & Schuster, 1996

From the Notebooks of Melanin Sun
by Jacqueline Woodson
Scholastic, 1995

The House You Pass on the Way
by Jacqueline Woodson
Delacorte, 1997

Hush
by Jacqueline Woodson
Penguin, 2002

I Hadn't Meant to Tell You This
by Jacqueline Woodson
Delacorte, 1994

Lena
by Jacqueline Woodson
Delacorte, 1999

Locomotion
by Jacqueline Woodson
Putnam, 2003

A Way Out of No Way: Writings About Growing Up Black in America
by Jacqueline Woodson
Henry Holt, 1996

American Dragons: Twenty-five Asian American Voices
edited by Laurence Yep
HarperCollins, 1993

Dragon's Gate
by Laurence Yep
HarperCollins, 1993

Dragonwings
by Laurence Yep
HarperCollins, 1975

Coolies
by Yin
illustrated by Chris K. Soentpiet
Penguin, 2001

Briar Rose
by Jane Yolen
Tor Books, 1992

Encounter
by Jane Yolen
illustrated by David Shannon
Harcourt, 1992

Sky Scrape/City Scape: Poems of City Life
selected by Jane Yolen
illustrated by Ken Condon
Boyds Mills, 1996

Armageddon Summer
by Jane Yolen and Bruce Coville
Harcourt, 1998

Appendix B: Young Adult Title List by Chapter

Chapter 1

The House on Mango Street
by Sandra Cisneros
Arte Publico, 1984

The Curious Incident of the Dog in the Night-Time
by Mark Haddon
Doubleday, 2003

The Bluest Eye
by Toni Morrison
Holt, Rinehart, and Winston, 1970

In Search of Our Mother's Gardens
by Alice Walker
Harcourt Brace Jovanovich, 1983

Chapter 2

Copper Sun
by Sharon Draper
Simon & Schuster, 2006

The Birchbark House
by Louise Erdrich
Hyperion, 1999

Nightjohn
by Gary Paulsen
Delacorte, 1993

Encounter
by Jane Yolen
illustrated by David Shannon
Harcourt, 1992

Chapter 3

None

Chapter 4

Navajo Code Talkers
by Nathan Aaseng
Walker, 1992

Bless Me, Ultima
by Rudolfo Anaya
Quinto Sol, 1972

Code Talker: A Novel About the Navajo Marines of World War Two
by Joseph Bruchac
Dial, 2005

The Heart of a Chief
by Joseph Bruchac
Dial, 1998

American Eyes: New Asian-American Short Stories for Young Adults
edited by Lori Marie Carlson
Henry Holt & Company, 1994

Moccasin Thunder: American Indian Stories for Today
edited by Lori Marie Carlson
HarperCollins, 2005

Who Will Tell My Brother?
by Marlene Carvell
Hyperion, 2002

Quinceañera Means Sweet 15
by Veronica Chambers
Hyperion, 2001

A Yellow Raft in Blue Water
by Michael Dorris
Henry Holt & Company, 1987

Unsung Heros of World War II: The Story of the Navajo Code Talkers
by Deanne Durrett
Facts on File, 1998

Love Medicine
by Louise Erdrich
Holt, 1984

Rising Voices: Writings of Young Native Americans
edited by Arlene Hirschfelder and Beverly R. Singer
Simon & Schuster, 1992

The Known World
by Edward P. Jones
Amistad, 2003

Warriors: Navajo Code Talkers
by Kenji Kawano
Northland Pub. Co, 1990

Quinceañera: Celebrating Fifteen
by Elizabeth King
Dutton, 1998

The Woman Warrior: Memoirs of a Girlhood Among Ghosts
by Maxine Hong Kingston
Knopf, 1976

Native Speaker
by Chang-Rae Lee
Riverhead, 1995

Beacon Hill Boys
by Ken Mochizuki
Scholastic, 2002

House Made of Dawn
by N. Scott Momaday
Harper, 1968

Cuba 15
by Nancy Osa
Random House, 2003
Select Awards & Honors: Pura Belpré Honor Book, An ALA Notable Book, An ALA Best Book for Young Adults, A *Booklist* Top Ten Youth First Novels

When the Emperor Was Divine
by Julie Otsuka
Knopf, 2002

Mixed: An Anthology of Short Fiction on the Multiracial Experience
edited by Chandra Prasad
W.W. Norton, 2006

Home of the Brave
by Allen Say
Houghton Mifflin, 2002

Ceremony
by Leslie Marmon Silko
Viking, 1977

Montana, 1948
by Larry Watson
Milkweed, 1993
Select Awards & Honors: 1993 Milkweed National Fiction Prize

A Suitcase Full of Seaweed and Other Stories
by Janet S. Wong
Simon & Schuster, 1996

A Way Out of No Way: Writings About Growing Up Black in America
by Jacqueline Woodson
Henry Holt, 1996

American Dragons: Twenty-five Asian American Voices
edited by Laurence Yep
HarperCollins, 1993

Dragonwings
by Laurence Yep
HarperCollins, 1975

Chapter 5

Dude! Stories and Stuff for Boys
edited by Sandy Asher and David L. Harrison
Penguin, 2006

On Her Way: Stories and Poems About Growing Up Girl
edited by Sandy Asher
Penguin, 2004

Am I Blue? Coming Out From the Silence
edited by Marion Dane Bauer
HarperCollins, 1994

Real Women Have Curves
Rating: PG 13
directed by Patricia Cardoso
screenplay by George Lavoo and Josefina Lopez
HBO Films, 2002
Select Awards & Honors: Audience Award at Sundance Film Festival 2002

Love and Sex: Ten Stories of Truth
edited by Michael Cart
Simon & Schuster, 2001

The House on Mango Street
by Sandra Cisneros
Arte Publico, 1984

Walk Two Moons
by Sharon Creech
HarperCollins, 1994

Party Girl
by Lynne Ewing
Alfred Knopf, 1998

Things I Have to Tell You: Poems and Writing by Teenage Girls
edited by Betsy Franco
photographs by Nina Nickles
Candlewick, 2001

You Hear Me? Poems and Writing by Teenage Boys
edited by Betsy Franco
photographs by Nina Nickles
Candlewick, 2000

Annie On My Mind
by Nancy Garden
Farrar, Straus and Giroux, 1982

Deliver Us from Evie
by M.E. Kerr
HarperCollins, 1994

The Woman Warrior: Memoirs of a Girlhood Among Ghosts
by Maxine Hong Kingston
Knopf, 1976

Boy Meets Boy
by David Levithan
Random House, 2003

Girls Got Game: Sports Stories and Poems
by Sue Macy
Henry Holt & Company, 2001

The Flip Side
by Andrew Matthews
Random House, 2003

Autobiography of My Dead Brother
by Walter Dean Myers
art by Christopher Myers
HarperCollins, 2005

Keeping You a Secret
by Julie Anne Peters
Little, Brown, 2003

Rainbow Boys
by Alex Sanchez
Simon & Schuster, 2001

Rainbow High
by Alex Sanchez
Simon & Schuster, 2003

Rainbow Road
by Alex Sanchez
Simon & Schuster, 2005

Guys Write for Guys Read
edited by Jon Scieszka
Viking Penguin, 2005

Like Sisters on the Homefront
by Rita Williams-Garcia
Lodestar, 1995

No Laughter Here
by Rita Williams-Garcia
HarperCollins, 2003

Hard Love
by Ellen Wittlinger
Simon & Schuster, 1999

Make Lemonade
by Virginia Euwer Wolff
Henry Holt, 1993

True Believer
by Virginia Euwer Wolff
Atheneum, 2001

From the Notebooks of Melanin Sun
by Jacqueline Woodson
Scholastic, 1995

The House You Pass on the Way
by Jacqueline Woodson
Delacorte, 1997

Chapter 6

With All My Heart, With All My Mind: Thirteen Stories About Growing Up Jewish
edited by Sandy Asher
Simon & Schuster, 1999

*Rock of Ages: A Tribute
to the Black Church*
by Tonya Bolden
illustrated by R. Gregory Christie
Random House, 2001

*Between Earth and Sky: Legends of
Native American Sacred Places*
by Joseph Bruchac
illustrated by Thomas Locker
Harcourt, 1996

Dark Sons
by Nikki Grimes
Hyperion, 2005

Witness
by Karen Hesse
Scholastic Press, 2001

Susannah
by Janet Hickman
Greenwillow Books, 1998

The Secret Life of Bees
by Sue Monk Kidd
Viking, 2002

*I Once Was a Monkey:
Stories Buddha Told*
by Jeanne M. Lee
Farrar, Straus and Giroux, 1999

Confessions of a Closet Catholic
by Sarah Darer Littman
Penguin, 2005

The Baptism
by Sheila P. Moses
Simon & Schuster, 2007

The Legend of Buddy Bush
by Sheila P. Moses
Margaret K. McElderry, 2003

The Return of Buddy Bush
by Sheila P. Moses
Margaret K. McElderry, 2005

Zen Shorts
by John Muth
Scholastic, 2005

Habibi
by Naomi Shihab Nye
Simon & Schuster, 1997

Buddha Book: A Meeting of Images
by Frank Olinksy
Diane Publishing, 1997

God Went to Beauty School
by Cynthia Rylant
HarperCollins, 2003

*I Believe in Water: Twelve Brushes
with Religion*
edited by Marilyn Singer
HarperCollins, 2000

Dust
by Arthur G. Slade
Random House, 2003

The Journey
by Sarah Stewart
illustrated by David Small
Farrar, Straus and Giroux, 2001

Sacred Places
by Philemon Sturges
illustrated by Giles Laroche
Penguin Young, 2000

Blankets
by Craig Thompson
Top Shelf, 2003

Hush
by Jacqueline Woodson
Penguin, 2002

Armageddon Summer
by Jane Yolen and Bruce Coville
Harcourt, 1998

Chapter 7

*Elegy on the Death of Cesar Chavez:
A Poem*
by Rudolfo Anaya
illustrated by Gaspar Enriquez
Cinco Puntos, 2000

The House on Mango Street
by Sandra Cisneros
Arte Publico, 1984

Growing Up Poor: A Literary Anthology
edited by Robert Coles and Randy
Testa with Michael Coles
New Press, 2001

Burning Up
by Caroline B. Cooney
Delacorte, 1999

Bucking the Sarge
by Christopher Paul Curtis
Random House, 2004

The Heart Knows Something Different:
Teenage Voices from the Foster Care
Ssystem: Youth Communication
edited by Al Desetta
Persea Books, 1996

Finding Fish: A Memoir
by Antwone Quenton Fisher, Mim
Eichler Rivas
Morrow, 2001

Seedfolks
by Paul Fleischman
HarperCollins, 1997

Crossing Jordan
by Adrian Fogelin
Peachtree, 2000

Pictures of Hollis Woods
by Patricia Reilly Giff
Random House, 2002
Select Awards & Honors: Newbery
Honor 2003, ALA Best Books for
Young Adults 2003, ALA Notable
Children's Books 2003

Breaking Through
by Francisco Jiménez
Houghton Mifflin, 2001

The Circuit: Stories from the Life of a
Migrant Child
by Francisco Jiménez
University of New Mexico Press, 1997

La Mariposa
by Francisco Jiménez
Houghton Mifflin, 1998

Soul Moon Soup
by Lindsay Lee Johnson
Boyds Mills, 1998

Kira-Kira
by Cynthia Kadohata
Simon & Schuster, 2004
Select Awards & Honors: John
Newbery Medal, Asian/Pacific
American Award for Literature

Spite Fences
by Trudy Krisher
Delacorte, 1994

Parrot in the Oven: Mi Vida
by Victor Martinez
HarperCollins, 1996

Chill Wind
by Janet McDonald
Farrar, Straus and Giroux, 2002

Twists and Turns
by Janet McDonald
Farrar, Straus and Giroux, 2003

The Glass Café or, The Stripper and
the State: How My Mother Started a
War With the System That Made Us
Kind of Rich and a Little Bit Famous
by Gary Paulsen
Random House, 2003

Esperanza Rising
by Pam Munoz Ryan
Scholastic, 2001

The Way a Door Closes
by Hope Anita Smith
illustrations by Shane W. Evans
Henry Holt, 2003

Sparrow
by Sherri L. Smith
Random House, 2006

Buried Onions
by Gary Soto
Harcourt, 1997

Learning the Game
by Kevin Waltman
Scholastic, 2005

I Hadn't Meant to Tell You This
by Jacqueline Woodson
Delacorte, 1994

Lena
by Jacqueline Woodson
Delacorte, 1999

Chapter 8

The Heart of a Chief
by Joseph Bruchac
Dial, 1998

The Tequila Worm
by Viola Canales
Random House, 2005

Walk Two Moons
by Sharon Creech
HarperCollins, 1994

Bang!
by Sharon Flake
Hyperion, 2005

Keesha's House
by Helen Frost
Farrar, Straus and Giroux, 2003

Spinning Through the Universe
by Helen Frost
Frances Foster, 2004

*Cinnamon Girl: Letters Found
Inside a Cereal Box*
by Juan Felipe Herrera
Joanna Cotler, 2005

Aleutian Sparrow
by Karen Hesse
Margaret K. McElderry, 2003

*Fishing for Chickens: Short Stories
About Rural Youth*
edited by Jim Heynen
Persea, 2001

The Brimstone Journals
by Ronald Koertge
Candlewick Press, 2001

Necessary Roughness
by Marie G. Lee
HarperCollins, 1996

My Chinatown
by Kam Max
HarperCollins, 2001

The Beast
by Walter Dean Myers
Scholastic, 2003

Shooter
by Walter Dean Myers
HarperCollins, 2004

Monster
by Walter Dean Myers
illustrated by Christopher Myers
HarperCollins, 1999

Come with Me: Poems for a Journey
by Naomi Shihab Nye
illustrated by Dan Yaccarino
Greenwillow, 2000

Music from a Place Called Half Moon
by Jerrie Oughton
Houghton Mifflin, 1995

Indian Shoes
by Cynthia Leitich Smith
HarperCollins, 2002

Rain Is Not My Indian Name
by Cynthia Leitich Smith
HarperCollins, 2001

Making Up Megaboy
by Virginia Walter
illustrated by Katrina Roeckelein
DK Publishing, 1998

*Big City Cool: Short Stories About
Urban Youth*
edited by M. Jerry Weiss and Helen S.
Weiss
Persea, 2002

Like Sisters on the Homefront
by Rita Williams-Garcia
Lodestar, 1995

Locomotion
by Jacqueline Woodson
Putnam, 2003

Sky Scrape/City Scape:
Poems of City Life
selected by Jane Yolen
illustrated by Ken Condon
Boyds Mills, 1996

Chapter 9

Finding Miracles
by Julia Alvarez
Alfred A. Knopf, 2004

How the Garcia Girls Lost Their Accents
by Julia Alvarez
Algonquin, 1991

How Tia Lola Came to Visit/Stay
by Julia Alvarez
Alfred A. Knopf, 2001

Navajo: Visions and Voices Across the
Mesa
by Shonto Begay
Scholastic, 1995

Cesar: ¡Si, Se Puede! (Yes, We Can!)
by Carmen T. Bernier-Grand
illustrated by David Diaz
Marshall Cavendish, 2004

Cool Salsa: Bilingual Poems on
Growing Up Hispanic in the
*United State*s
edited by Lori M. Carlson
Henry Holt, 1994

Red Hot Salsa: Bilingual Poems
on Being Young and Latino
in the United States
edited by Lori M. Carlson
Henry Holt, 2005

Marisol and Magdalena: The Sound
of our Sisterhood
by Veronica Chambers
Hyperion, 1998

Shanghai Messenger
by Andrea Cheng
illustrated by Ed Young
Lee & Low, 2005

Copper Sun
by Sharon Draper
Simon & Schuster, 2006

First Crossing: Stories About Teen
Immigrants
by Donald R. Gallo
Candlewick Press, 2004

Maggie's Door
by Patricia Reilly Giff
Random House, 2003

Letters from Rifka
by Karen Hesse
Henry Holt, 1992
Select Awards & Honors: National
Jewish Book Award, Sydney Taylor
Book Award, Christopher Book Award

Born Confused
by Tanuja Desai Hidier
Scholastic, 2002

Naming Maya
by Uma Krishnaswami
Farrar, Straus and Giroux, 2004

A Step from Heaven
by An Na
Boyds Mills Press, 2001

The Good Rainbow Road
by Simon J. Ortiz
illustrated by Michael Lacapa
translated by Victor Montejo
University of Arizona Press, 2004

Yellow Star
by Jennifer Roy
Marshall Cavendish, 2006

Tangled Threads: A Hmong
*Girl's Stor*y
by Pegi Deitz Shea
Houghton Mifflin, 2003

Blue Jasmine
by Kashmira Sheth
Hyperion, 2004

Neighborhood Odes
by Gary Soto
illustrated by David Diaz
Harcourt, 1992

Wachale! Poetry and Prose About
Growing Up Latino in America
edited by Ilan Stavans
Cricket Books, 2001

Chapter 10

A Movie in My Pillow/Una Pelicula
en Mi Almohada
by Jorge Argueta
illustrated by Elizabeth Gómez
Children's Book Press, 2001

Hidden Roots
by Joseph Bruchac
Scholastic, 2004

The Birchbook House
by Louise Erdrich
Hyperion, 1999

Breeding Better Vermonters: The
Eugenics Project in the Green
Mountain State
by Nancy L Gallagher
University Press of New England, 1999

Fat Kid Rules the World
by K. L. Going
Penguin, 2003

Out of the Dust
by Karen Hesse
Scholastic, 1997

Angela Johnson: Poetic Prose
by KaaVonia Hinton
Rowman & Littlefield, 2006

Farewell to Manzanar: A True Story
of Japanese American Experience
During and After the World War II
Internment
by Jeanne Wakatsuki Houston and
James D. Houston
Houghton Mifflin, 1973

The First Part Last
by Angela Johnson
Simon & Schuster, 2003
Select Awards & Honors: Coretta
Scott King Award, Michael L. Printz
Award

Heaven
by Angela Johnson
Simon & Schuster, 1998

Still I Rise: A Cartoon History of
African Americans
by Roland Owen Laird and
Taneshia Laird
illustrated by Elihu Bey
W.W. Norton, 1997

When the Levees Broke: A Requim
in Four Acts
directed by Spike Lee
HBO, 2006

Looking for Alibrandi
by Melina Marchetta
Orchard, 1999

The Tuskegee Airmen
directed by Robert Markowitz
HBO Films, 1995

Baseball Saved Us
by Ken Mochizuki
Lee & Low, 1993

I, Dred Scott: A Fictional Slave
Narrative Based on the Life and
Legal Precedent of Dred Scott
by Sheila P. Moses
Simon & Schuster, 2005

Patrol: An American Soldier in
Vietnam
by Walter Dean Myers
HarperCollins, 2002

Carver: A Life in Poems
by Marilyn Nelson
Boyds Mills, 1997
Select Awards & Honors: John
Newbery Honor Award, Coretta Scott
King Honor Award

Project Mulberry: A Novel
by Linda Sue Park
Clarion Books, 2005

Esperanza Rising
by Pam Munoz Ryan
Scholastic, 2001

Milkweed
by Jerry Spinelli
Random House, 2003

The Black Brothers
by Lisa Tetzner
illustrated by Hannes Binder
Boyds Mills Press, 2004

Bat 6
by Virginia Euwer Wolff
Scholastic, 1998

Being the Wheel: Poems about Driving
by Janet Wong
Margaret K. McElderry, 1999

Dragon's Gate
by Laurence Yep
HarperCollins, 1993

Dragonwings
by Laurence Yep
HarperCollins, 1975

Coolies
by Yin
illustrated by Chris K. Soentpiet
Penguin, 2001

Briar Rose
by Jane Yolen
Tor Books, 1992

Chapter 11

Whale Talk
by Chris Crutcher
Greenwillow, 2001

The Contender
by Robert Lipsyte
Harper, 1967

Picture of Hollis Woods
by Patricia Reilly Giff
Random House, 2002

The Great Gilly Hopkins
by Katherine Patterson
HarperCollins, 1978

Chapter 12

None

Appendix C: Selected Audio Books

Walk Two Moons, by Sharon Creech, read by Kate Harper, Listening Library, 1997.

Whale Talk, by Chris Crutcher, read by Brian Corrigan, Listening Library, 2002.

A Yellow Raft in Blue Water, by Michael Dorris, read by Barbara Rosenblat, Audio Bookshelf, 2003.

Forged by Fire, by Sharon M. Draper, read by Thomas Penny, Recorded Books, 2002.

A companion to *Tears of a Tiger*, the novel describes Gerald's impoverished and abusive childhood.

Keesha's House, by Helen Frost, narrated by multiple readers, Recorded Books, 2004.

Written in poetry, several teens struggle with challenges such as pregnancy, homophobia, and homelessness.

Maggie's Door, by Patricia Reilly Giff, read by Fionnula Flanagan, Listening Library, 2003.

Companion to *Nory Ryan's Song*, Nory and friend Sean Red Mallon travel from Ireland to New York despite financial difficulties and hunger.

* *Pictures of Hollis Woods*, by Patricia Reilly Giff, read by Hope Davis, Listening Library, 2002.

Fat Kid Rules the World, by K. L. Going, read by Matthew Lillard, Listening Library, 2003.

Aleutian Sparrow, by Karen Hesse, narrated by Sarah Jones, Listening Library, 2003.

Out of the Dust, by Karen Hesse, read by Martha Mashburn, Listening Library, 1998.

The First Part Last, by Angela Johnson, narrated by Khalipa Oldjohn and Kole Kristi, Listening Library, 2004.

The Poisonwood Bible, by Barbara Kingsolver, read by Dean Robertson, Brilliance Audio, 2004.

Set from 1959 to the 1990s, the book explores the Price family's sojourn in Africa.

Spite Fences, by Trudy Krisher, read by Kate Forbes, Recorded Books, 2001.

Looking for Alibrandi, by Melina Marchetta, read by Marcella Russo, Bolinda Audio, 1999.

Parrot in the Oven: Mi Vida, by Victor Martinez, read by the author, Harper Audio, 1998.

Shooter, by Walter Dean Myers, narrated by Chad Coleman, Bernie McInerny, and Michelle Santopietro, Recorded Books, 2004.

A Step from Heaven, by An Na, read by Jina Oh, Listening Library, 2002.

Habibi, by Naomi Shihab Nye, read by Chistina Moore, Recorded Books, 1999.

Project Mulberry, by Linda Sue Park, read by Mina Kim, Listening Library, 2005.

The Chosen, by Chaim Potok, read by Jonathan Davis, Recorded Books, 2003.

Set in Brooklyn, the protagonist, Danny Saunders, has been chosen to take on his father's role as *tzaddik*, a spiritual leader and advisor, but he is more interested in learning about secular matters explored by his friend Reuven Malters.

*Esperanza Rising, by Pam Munoz Ryan, read by Trini Alvarado, Listening Library, 2001.

Lizzie Bright and the Buckminster Boy, by Gary D. Schmidt, read by Sam Freed, Random House, 2005.

Turner Buckminster befriends Lizzie Bright, an African American, though citizens of their Maine community, including Turner's dad who is a minister, are prejudice and plan to evict Lizzie and her family from their island.

*Buried Onions, by Gary Soto, read by Robert Ramirez, Recorded Books, 2001.

*Milkweed, by Jerry Spinelli, narrated by Ron Rifkin, Listening Library, 2003.

The Land, by Mildred D. Taylor, read by Ruben Santiago-Hudson, Listening Library, 2001.

In this prequel to *Roll of Thunder, Hear My Cry*, Cassie Logan's grandfather, Paul-Edward Logan tries to make a home for himself and the family he hopes to have some day.

Make Lemonade, by Virginia Euwer Wolff, read by Heather Alicia Simms, Listening Library, 2002.

Determined to attend college, LaVaughn gets a job babysitting Jeremy and Jilly, seventeen-year-old Jolly's two children.

*True Believer, by Virginia Euwer Wolff, read by Heather Alicia Simms, Listening Library, 2002.

*Lena, by Jacqueline Woodson, read by Kate Forbes, Recorded Books, 1999.

Miracle's Boys, by Jacqueline Woodson, read by Dule Hill, Listening Library, 2001.

Set in New York, the Bailey household changes when Charlie returns home from a detention center to live with his two brothers, 22-year-old Tyree and 12-year-old Lafayette.

*Used in the text.

Index